KRISIA'S SILENCE

THE GIRL WHO WAS NOT ON SCHINDLER'S LIST

RONNY HEIN

ISBN 9789493231399 (ebook)

ISBN 9789493231382 (paperback)

ISBN 9789493231443 (hardcover)

Publisher: Amsterdam Publishers, The Netherlands

info@amsterdampublishers.com

Krisia's Silence is Book 13 in the series :

Holocaust Survivor True Stories WWII

Copyright © Ronny Hein, 2021

Original title: O silêncio de Krisia

English translation: Jane Adlington

Cover image: Auschwitz, Poland (via depositphotos.com) with insert Krisia Perlberger, circa 1939

CONTENTS

INTRODUCTION
THE WAR RETOLD

On 8 January 1996, a wet Monday in São Paulo, Krystyna Hein, formerly Krisia Perlberger, also known as Krisiu, Krysia and other variations, all derived from Polish, gave her testimony to the team at the Shoah Foundation, at the University of Southern California, known then as Survivors of the Shoah Visual History Foundation.

The institution had been founded by Steven Spielberg two years earlier. No other Hollywood director or movie producer has had so many productions listed among the 100 best films in the entire history of cinema. He has won dozens of awards for his creative work; he won the Oscar for Best Film for 'Schindler's List', made in 1993 and considered to be his masterpiece. And this is not his only Oscar.

Spielberg became so emotionally involved with his own film that he decided to set up an institution to collect the testimonies of the last survivors of the Holocaust. It was a brilliant and viable idea for a wealthy, well-connected man. Thousands of victims from several countries were able to tell their personal experience. Some of them lived in a nation that had built apparently limitless power, persuading its citizens that there were inferior beings in their midst whose summary removal would bring peace and prosperity to the empire, that would then last for a thousand years and would spread across continents.

Given that in 1995, 40 years had passed since Germany's defeat, presumably thousands of people between 60 and 70 years of age still had a personal contribution to give to the world in helping elucidate the cliched maxim that those who learn from history will be condemned to repeat it.

This is a nice sounding axiom of little practical relevance. If history has taught its observers anything over the centuries, sadly it is that people will more readily preserve the memory of their religion, bigotry and ideology than the pain and shame that should be kept alive in our minds. It is worth noting too that ignorance is always more powerful and effective than knowledge. Testimonies, dismissed as old people, are not considered indicative and tend to be undermined by generations that have broken new ground and are therefore disparaging of the values and ills that afflicted their predecessors.

Clearly there will be people who will contest these lessons, although curiously, a minister of the Brazilian state emulated Joseph Goebbels himself on national television in January 2020. The poor man, relieved of his post the very next day, did not even have time to understand what he had done. Some considered him to be a neo-Nazi or something similar. I do not believe this was the case. The young clown was simply following a script without evaluating, either before or after, the meaning of what he was saying nor the role he was playing. I dare say that if he had actually come face to face with Goebbels, he would have been scared witless.

However, we should see the testimonies provided to the Shoah Foundation through different eyes. Technological advances alone have made it possible and economically viable to transform separate interviews into a reasonably precise patchwork of what happened in those years, the subtlety and opprobrium of each humiliation, the guilt, the innocence and the supposed heroism of some people. Heroism, that may or may not be justified, having been won by trading in people's freedom.

If it is true that history is the story of the winners and therefore it is distorted by them, the same cannot be said when events are narrated by the victims, above all when they have no political intentions. Victims simply tell their stories. Underlying their words are sensations of pain and hatred, notwithstanding exaggerations and omissions due to memory lapses, of course.

Anyone who sees the survivors' testimonies is certainly party to true stories. Tone of voice, tears shed and body language help clarify understanding and doubt about what is being said. The more that people tell their own stories and the more comparisons interested parties can draw, the greater the chance of nearing the truth.

As with research based on samples, the larger the accumulation, the lower the margin of error to the point where it reaches near insignificance.

When I read some of the interviews that helped with producing this book, I realised, however, that the attitude of each one of the survivors would never allow for a sense of harmony or hegemony in the accounts. Some talk a great deal, some brush over the details, some remember so much and some hardly anything at all. This is just the way people are, with or without wars.

What Spielberg did – possibly his greatest legacy, despite some brilliant films – was to create a retelling of the war, not by winners or by losers. The war told by those who suffered it. From now on, somehow, there will always be witnesses during wars, unless all the victims perish or decide to be silent once the war has ended.

In the future, if a compilation is made quickly enough of all that remains, it will not be acceptable for an international court such as the one held in Nüremberg to lead to a total of only 12 death sentences, for millions of murders carried out without any military 'justification'. This is the precise number of perpetrators hanged for the biggest act of extermination ever carried out.

In the future, the story told by Krystyna Hein, aged 64, in her short and, in some sense, neutral testimony of January 1996, will be equally important to her children and grandchildren living in a country she did not know in her childhood, as will those told by other survivors whose experiences of the war were shorter (although never less painful) but whose video accounts go on for four, five or six hours.

Her stories are in this book, along with speculations, gaps filled by mere logic and conclusions reached through research. In the stories told here are accounts by others. They were linked to the most tragic, complex and pertinent event of the 20th century. These were chosen by the author on the condition that I had to personally meet and evaluate each of the sources myself.

I postponed writing on this subject for decades. I concluded, perhaps precipitously, that even if I did so, I'd have nothing to add to this story, which has been told so many times that it has become a cliché and has lost most of meaning.

I once wrote that all paradises have lost their meaning because of the simple fact that the terms 'paradise' and 'paradisiac' have been used with such lack of criteria and hierarchy that there is simply no way to distinguish the coral reefs of Polynesia and Indian waterways from any old fetid strip of sand around the world. Nowadays, paradise is an expression used by people selling car parts or sweets made from corn.

The Holocaust, with a capital H or entirely upper case, has become sadly commonplace.

If this book falls into the common grave of war stories, there will be nothing I can do, except, perhaps surrender to the conclusion that I wrote another useless piece of work about the least paradisiac time in recent history.

However, when I see a few elderly people crying at the commemoration of 75 years since the end of the extermination camp at Auschwitz, I realise that telling the story of some of these people is the best I can do.

Krystyna told her story to the Shoah Foundation, but it is shallow like a muddy river. It is my duty to dig deeper because I am her son, and she departed before we had time to talk, or at least I think so. This is an assumption about which we sadly never spoke.

In the interview for Spielberg, we see a well-groomed woman who looks uninhibited and seems to be in a curiously good mood. At the end, the camera operator moves round to bring Sven, my father, into the frame.

The interviewer immediately asks Krisia to introduce him. Sven was sitting in a wheelchair, not having as happy a life as he deserved.

"This is Sven," she says frankly. "He has been my companion for 42 years (43 in May). He makes my life bearable."

Bear-ab-le was what she said, quite naturally.

It was only then that I understood how intolerable it was for this woman to live with her memories and circumstances.

This is what war does.

A PRISONER OF TIME

At the end, nothing interested her. Only time. She did not even remember her grandchildren's names or what she had done in her life, which had been both intense and inexplicable. Perhaps unacceptable would be a better word. But she still had time. She looked into her lap while day after day the dull colourless screen showed tennis matches, the only lure from the past that could possibly reconnect her to the world. She had been happy on the courts, neither competitive nor special – just happy. There was a ball to keep track of, a yellow sphere that bounced confidently, because something – the scoreboard, the voices of the players or the summer sweat – made sense.

Or did they?

What about time?

She never moved from the sofa from where she wanted to keep track of time. If anybody forgot to put on her wrist-watch, she would complain, and her fragile yet demanding voice would travel down the long corridor to anyone within earshot. And whoever heard her would hurry to fetch her watch from the drawer next to her. The watch was made by Champion. It was an analogue and had to be swapped for another with bigger hands whenever her eyesight grew dimmer. Once it was on her narrow wrist, she would gaze silently at it. She never said the hour, the minute or the day, though she would glance at it often.

In these moments, I would look on with the most intense love of all, I, her son, and her daughter, when she could come, as she lived far away. In some strange way, I was able to plunge into time and travel with her anywhere. Whether we were together, sharing the moment, I will never know.

Of all my interactions with her over the years, nothing seemed more important to me than this time we spent together. Not even the stories from Yugoslavia she read to me when I was a child or the 73 letters she wrote to me on 73 consecutive days when I was homesick on a trip I made in my youth (I was the one who wrote first, of course, but she wanted me to tell her all about it, and she reciprocated). Not even her demands for me to get good grades or the silence she proffered seemed more important to me.

Of course she was absent, but somehow we were connected. I would teasingly call her "Silly Mum". She would usually respond, "Silly boy", and she did so for the rest of her life. To transport her further into the journeys in her brain, which I had seen empty and undefined on a scan, I would sometimes sing the sentence to a simple tune. And the reward of hearing her sing with me, in time, made everything worthwhile.

Especially coming from her, as she had never been able to sing. I do not know whether this lack of musical perception was the product of the years she had spent imprisoned when she was just a child. Someone told me that this was not the case, that people are either born with an ability to distinguish musical pitch or not. It comes down to either God or DNA. But I remember that when we used to sing on the veranda in Mairinque, accompanied by Margareth's guitar, with my father's harmonica and the light of the moon, her voice could not be heard. A music teacher and renowned maestro of the American school where she learned to read at 16 (it was only then that she had the opportunity) had the task of getting her to participate in the class choir for the end-of-year presentation. But no amount of instruction worked. She was tone-deaf. So the maestro had a practical idea: "Please, make no sound. Just move your lips during rehearsals and the presentation." It worked. Silence was her speciality. It was this, in all its forms, that saved her life in the six years she was in the ghettos or at the mercy of tormentors in the concentration camps.

Maybe – I suggest without any kind of scientific conviction – her obsession with wristwatches harkened back to those days. Perhaps she wondered how long it would be until it would all be over. Or starting over. In places such as those she had been held, only shouting and orders marked the passing of the days and the minutes. Of course, every day there would be new absences. People would disappear to who knows where. Her mother, who was by her side during those long years of deprivation of liberty, may have been responsible for her silences. She told my mom never to have contact with other people because if she became attached, there would be the chance she would feel the pain of loss. And if she said the wrong thing, she might experience the pain of the lash – or worse, of separation.

All that is left to me and the few people who knew her before her second death (survivors, we know, die at least twice) are her memories, which were neither intense nor particularly factual.

2

FRUITLESS FRUIT

She did not know the name of the ship that brought her to Santos from Scandinavia or Germany. I just know that when she was collected, she was alone. Her mother had died of typhoid close to peace being declared. A Red Cross worker decided that Krisia had to be sent to a sanatorium in Sweden. Another unsourced reference – perhaps from that night in my childhood that I will talk about later – led me to believe that long-limbed Krisia weighed 26 kilos when freed by British soldiers. She was sick, undernourished and consumptive.

I assume she made the journey to that Nordic town in a state of near delirium. Cloudy images, unfamiliar voices and strange languages. On the way, someone was kind enough to gently feed her. It is a known fact that the soldiers, who freed the frail prisoners, were moved and gave them bars of chocolate and tins of food. In many cases, the rich nutrients in the soldiers' rations ended up killing the survivors, giving them terrible dysentery.

What more did she tell me?

That the Swedish nurses were kind nuns. That it took a long time for her to manage any kind of communication with her caretakers. This was not a problem given that she continued to practice silence as her rule of life. Gradually, after about six months to a year, her convalescence drew to an end. New flesh covered her bones, and her skin tone began to brighten. Her eyes were no longer apathetic.

But what was going through her mind? I never met any of those angels who helped her return from death, so I was never able to ask them about how she behaved. Did she cry? I do not think so. During the remainder of her survival years, my mother was never one to cry. Did she get upset? Did she tremble? What went through the mind of a girl without relatives, points of reference or affection?

I do not know whether there were other girls in a similar condition in the sanatorium in Malmö, but it is impossible to imagine she would have grown close to any of them. Being forgotten in a corner had been a blessing in the previous years. Stay, go over there. But to be forgotten by everyone? To realise there was nobody in the vast world of ruins that Europe had become, not a single soul, who knew she existed or cared that she did? She was like a piece of fruit that had fallen from a forgotten tree in a corner of the forest. To make matters worse, winter had fallen, and not even the birds and insects knew of her existence.

These valleys stretched out across the geography of my growing years. I slowly started to understand that the mind fills these spaces with a strange mortar that ends up being worn away by torrents that stem from doubt, bitterness and horrific experiences.

I would have liked to have asked, but my father forbade discussing issues surrounding the memory of pain. He was born in Berlin, Germany, but had been taken away from there by his cautious parents when Hitler rose to power. He spent the war years in Brazil, far from the bombing and ethnic persecution. He believed, therefore, that not bringing up his wife's suffering was a way of easing it. Some people condemned him for this. They said that Krisia should tell everything, to free herself of her past, to exorcise it – if possible.

I disagree. Being my parents' son, I have known many survivors of the war. Some spoke about this subject all the time. They remembered, they forgot, they told stories that they had probably made up, although they did not realise it, given that they almost always contained new details or omitted previous ones.

Once, in a restaurant, the charming name of which was *Kis Pipa* (Small Pipe) in Budapest, I was party to an incomprehensible conversation between two unusual individuals, two people who had been released from Auschwitz. They were together until freed by North American soldiers on a filthy train in Germany. One of them was my father-in-law, a prisoner who never practiced silence. The other was called Luís, usually known as Lóli. After an exchange that started out affectionately, they both became agitated. I had no idea whether they were talking about football, politics or women – Hungarian is called the devil's language because of its hermetic structure – but at one point I thought they were going to start fighting. Chairs were flying, blood dripping, and of course it ended in tears and an exchange of hugs, the kind to be expected of those who had shared the experience of the terror of pursuit. I soon learned that the subject was, in fact, the war. And the reason for the disagreement had been their divergent memories. Luís remembered a story. André, my father-in-law, remembered it differently.

This is why I see no difference between constantly recalling everything and never remembering anything. Being silent or repeating. Wounds are not expelled through the mouth, nor do they hurt more for those who cling to them. Those who continue to live are forever burdened with a mysterious pain, whether this is false or true.

3

THE NIGHT SHE BROKE THE SILENCE

On a timeless night of my childhood – I do not know whether it was cold or hot, nor do I remember whether we were in one of the bedrooms or in the living room – my mother decided to tell us "everything" she remembered. The quotes for "everything" are meant to underline that her memories were vague.

She announced that she did not like to talk about the issue, so that would be the only time that we, her children, would have the chance to plunge into the depths of her intangible past. I think my father was in another room and had agreed to her rummaging in her box of sad memories, at least that time. I heard everything silently. I must have cried because I always cry, but the few brushstrokes that were recorded on my memory canvas have never lived up to what was said.

Years later, Krisia was invited to give her account to be included in a virtual museum, the Shoah Foundation, created by Steven Spielberg to save words from the Holocaust – as it was too late to save lives. Her testimony, dreary and dry, lasted less than 40 minutes. Forty minutes to account for six years of destitution. It contained no details –

not a shadow of the detailed prose she had used in the 73 letters she wrote me that I have already mentioned. Maybe she did not remember anything else – or anything that could be told. Maybe she wanted to keep the essential details to herself. I remember the narrative she recorded better than the one I'd heard during my childhood. However, other facts, true or false, from that single night in my childhood were erased.

Because I make a living from writing, I have been asked several times to write the story of my mother and other survivors with whom I lived. Countless stories exist – some full of cowardice, some of vindictive memories.

During my life, I have read dozens of works on the inexplicable carnage of those years. Most of them are weak and poorly written. Others are piercing and cut my veins and tissues. Gradually I began to believe that the value of these memories is almost nothing given the inevitable conclusion that this is the history of humankind (in lower caps), a weird species that was given the gift of never learning from experience.

Never before have I seriously thought about redoing what has already been done. It is said that the repetition of memory prevents the repetition of events. This, everyone knows, is nonsense.

Krisia left her life when she could no longer wind the spring on her wristwatch. Her death reminded me of everything I knew or assumed I had known and urged me to write these lines as a tribute to her memory, even though the story does not add anything to the war chronicle that has been repeated so often it has become empty – as occurs with some words that are used so often that they become meaningless clichés.

Few were present at her funeral on a hot and sunny day – the type of weather she had always loathed. Almost everyone – including my father – had died before her, in the early years of the 21st century. When it was my time to throw earth onto her casket – an agonizing tradition of Jewish funerals – I called her "Silly Mum" once more. Of course she did not hear me. Nor did she answer, as, inexplicably, she had answered just the morning before. There was a rabbi and a liturgical singer, both flanking the unburied casket. On the lid of the casket, made of quickly recyclable wood, was the same Star of David that, for years, had identified her as an outcast of her time and place.

The Star of David, also known – who knows why – as Shield of David, is a reminder of Israel's second king in antiquity and identifies the followers of Judaism. My mother and her close ancestors were not religious. My father's relatives were even less connected to religion than my mother's were. As time passed, the Jews on my father's side had become part of German life, barely remembering their origins.

Hitler's antisemitism – like that practiced throughout the ages – managed to revive a dim light of religion in some of its victims.

In the previous sentence, religion would have to be replaced by origin, as persecution has always had stronger roots in ethnicity than in faith. It never occurred to the executioners from different eras that Jews would probably have disappeared by assimilation. This did not happen because of so many events that ended up bringing them together over time.

As a child, Krisia never lived in a Jewish neighbourhood or followed special dietary rules. In her childhood home, no one separated the dishes and cutlery that were used for meat and dairy, a principle backed by *kashrut*, the set of dietary rules ordered by the rabbis for the followers of the Torah, the sacred books of Judaism. She did not remember going to the synagogue in Krakow – her hometown – except for the luxurious wedding ceremony of an aunt, who was driven to the local synagogue in a carriage drawn by beautiful and unforgettable horses.

Krisia, therefore, was not a religious Jew during her childhood. And she only occasionally attended synagogue many years after the war had ended. Her visits to the synagogue were as scarce as her faith. She just insisted on being present on Yom Kippur, the day of forgiveness, the most sacred date of Judaism, always subsequent to the beginning of the new year (Rosh Hashanah) on the Jewish calendar. She used Yom Kippur to revere her dead ancestors, including her mother who had died in the Bergen-Belsen concentration camp, on the very day of its liberation. To fulfil the Jewish ritual, she followed a 24-hour fast as a way to ask for forgiveness for something. She never knew what. I have to add here that abstaining from food and drink – not even sips of water were allowed that day – never bothered her. In fact, Krisia missed only her cigarettes, as she smoked three packs a day until she was 60 years old.

Clearly, she was never religious. She was buried in a Jewish cemetery for only two reasons, and they were not related to belief in the resurrection or any other religious aspect. The first reason relates to my father. Quiescent, as always, she ended up being taken along the same path as her husband 18 years earlier and reached him through an underground pipeline. She was unaware of the second reason. She never expressed a desire *not* to be incinerated – another possible destiny for her body at the end. This decision was made by us, her children, for the simple reason that we felt uncomfortable about setting fire to a person who had so fiercely resisted the criminal cremation practiced by those who had persecuted her.

The cemetery is a lush green area, like the parks and gardens at the latitude of the Tropic of Capricorn, with discreet headstones carrying Hebrew inscriptions and symbols related to the history of the Jewish people. There is rain and heat in adequate doses, not a single snowflake and just the right amount of cold necessary to keep the grass healthy and green.

In Malmö, the forests only thrive in the few months of the year when the sun shines weakly. Winds push the temperatures down to less than minus 20 degrees in the winter, which is why there are numerous bars close to the port for dock workers to seek a little heat. The city has survived for centuries on business related to the dock. Nowadays, it also relies on the fares and tariffs charged to cross the Ore canal, that connects Sweden and Denmark. This is an intricate set of bridges and tunnels that did not exist in Krisia's time.

I sometimes wonder what would have happened to her if, after six months – or maybe a year – of healing in Malmö, she had been shown the door of the clinic, without the slightest idea of where to go. Prisoners tend to return to their homes, and so do war survivors.

But where was that 15-year-old girl's home in 1946? In her hometown of Krakow, which she barely remembered and had left as a child? And who would she have looked up there? The grandparents and uncles she would remember only later no longer lived there. Some had fled to different parts of the world while they could. Others, like her, had been caught by invading troops. Many perished during the conflict, like her mother. Her father was certainly no longer among the living. A lawyer ranked as a major early in the war, he had said that the Germans would never be able to beat the Polish army. He said that and then left for battle on his horse. It was an unfortunate patriotic battle cry. Only one or two days later, Poland was transformed into a land of smoke and blood and was brought to its knees by the enemy.

4

A CROSS TO BEAR

If not Poland, then where? Which path could a young, not particularly healthy, illiterate young women take? She had no professional training and did not speak the local language.

Here I will leave room for the usual speculations. These may produce both shallow TV shows or edifying testimonials, so many of which are gathered at the end of every war, the material of cliché and easy, fleeting tears that obscure the past, leaving it forgotten on dusty bookshelves or in digital archives rendered obsolete by fast-moving technology.

I am raising this issue merely as an opportunity to learn something. I believe in the importance of speculating on the paths down which terror could have led its victims.

My mother's path was a different one and involved the frenetic pages of the New York newspapers that thrived after the war. America was triumphant, Europe's victors were still in tatters and mountains of recriminations were yet to be cleared from the paths ahead.

The mission of the International Red Cross, founded in 1863 by Henry Dunant, now present in 190 countries under different names (Red Crescent in Muslim countries, Magen David Adom in Israel), is to "protect the life and dignity of victims of armed conflict and other violent situations and to provide assistance". There are those who have questioned the integrity of some of its actions and management over the years, but the decisive role it played in Krisia's life is undeniable.

After taking her in, sheltering her and sending her on her way at the end of the Second World War, the institution played other unexpected and determining roles in her life. The harrowing scene of her leaving the sanatorium with nowhere to go never arose. The image of a piece of fruit at the foot of an abandoned tree in the corner of a frozen forest was also kept at bay because of what ensued.

One morning, as he probably did every day, a balding man called Tovek bought a paper at a newsstand on a street corner in New York. The family says that the publication was *The New York Times* – although it could have been a different one. Nobody saw or checked. I assume that Tovek lived in Brooklyn, as he was Jewish. A member of the family who was rather fancy, so never invented stories involving poverty, told me on one occasion that Tovek lived on the Upper East Side, an upmarket part of town.

Tovek was her uncle, and my mother's uncle and his address is of no consequence. The point is that he must have opened his newspaper to see what was happening in the post-war world and possibly to discover whether any new benefit for foreign refugees was bubbling in the pipeline of the United States of America's agenda. It was said that of my mother's seven uncles, Jakub Tobiaz (his real name) was the one who lived in the most precarious conditions and, therefore, really needed any help the authorities decided to make available. This was never discussed within earshot of the fancy relative, but it was assumed that this was a true story.

Anyway, it so happened that on that particular day, the International Red Cross had published a full-spread list of survivors, set out in alphabetical order. The list was published in other newspapers widely circulated around the planet. Above all, it was a lifeline for those who still held out hope of finding family members presumed to have been killed during the war years.

I was told that many refugees from Europe did not even bother looking over the Red Cross lists. Almost everyone had a clear idea of the murderous diligent fury with which Hitler's army had done away with its victims. They were efficient, merciless people. To escape from that was as unlikely as winning the lottery, and let's face it, few people would waste their time checking a list of winners of competitions that are almost impossible to win. It is difficult to know whether Tovek was looking through the list through mere curiosity or whether he actually expected to find someone who had disappeared, a needle in a haystack.

My own personal hypothesis was always to cherish my conviction that Tovek was actually looking for his niece Krisia. On the rare days that she brought up old memories, she would sometimes mention that Uncle Tovek used to call her by the nickname "Kisha Pélele", a play on words of the kind that works in any language. This was an affectionate, avuncular way of making a child called Krisia Perlberger happy. In Krakow, whole families lived in houses grouped in a U shape. I saw this much later. It was reminiscent of a castle, taking up a whole cul-de-sac. It was quite plausible that a person like Tovek would look for the name of a little girl he had never seen, on a Red Cross list. Maybe I am being fanciful, but for now I am standing by my story until proven wrong, and I am afraid there is not a person alive who could do that.

For an image to leap from the cold letters of a newspaper and come back to life in someone's memory is akin to the miracle of birth. And so it was that a bedridden being in Sweden, visited only by nuns at scheduled times, a girl lost in an ugly, disfigured world, became significant again. Like newborn babies who arrive from nowhere and turn into people.

To re-exist (or exist again) is not as simple as it may seem. I do not know what it was like for her or when the news that somebody had found her reached the Scandinavian hospital. I assume that, if she were a whole person, which she would never be again, the information that a relative had managed to locate her would have been cause for celebration. I do not, however, believe that there would have been any pretence of festive spirit in the sanatorium where my mother was convalescing.

Many years after this, I saw on many occasions that nothing unnerved her more than the prospect of some kind of change. Any change in the circumstances to which she had become accustomed, whatever they were, would lead to panic, bad moods, excessive complaining and tearless sobbing, her personal way of breaking down. Some such cases to back me up exist. The most recent was as meaningful as it was incomprehensible to anyone who did not know her. Years after my father's death, Krisia reluctantly agreed to leave the solitude of her big house in Campos do Jordão, which was unsuitable for an elderly person to live in, particularly as she showed no interest in seeing the old friends who used to visit. We managed to convince her to move to an apartment in an area of São Paulo where she knew a number of people.

She had lived in the house in the mountains with her husband in his final years and was only convinced to give it up when offered an apartment with air conditioning throughout. Ah, cool air, at least there was cool air, even if it was artificial. This did not have the desired effect.

As she had in her previous home, my mother isolated herself from the world. She consented to a weekly stroll with my sister – as long as it was short and had a clear purpose, to buy bread, for example. For a while, her grandson kept her company, but not even this, or the fact that she was extremely fond of the little boy, brought her any detectable joy.

She spent the days with Dolly, her white poodle, sitting on the sofa watching television. She would neither accept invitations nor reciprocate, not even for the sake of being polite. She went back to being the silent woman she had been in hospital. In this period, some people who did not know Krisia very well thought her bad-tempered, unpleasant even, and not without cause.

The truth, however, is that throughout her long second life in Brazil, she kept the defensive or aggressive tone that had got her through her years in captivity. But it was just a question of peeling away the outer layers (kindly, of course), revealing the sweet fruit hidden by rough skin.

The allegory is not particularly creative, but it was entirely appropriate in describing Krisia, who appeared tough in the beginning but softened after some time. Obviously, this duality changed over time and in different circumstances. In hard times, her bad-temperedness thickened to the width of a castle wall. In good times, her sweet nature flowed like water from a spring on a rainy day.

Once the family realised that this new solitude in São Paulo was damaging her both emotionally and in more concrete ways (it seems one of her carers took several of her not particularly valuable material treasures, like jewellery, watches and money), and as I was about to move to a more spacious place, one with a leafy garden and solid foundations built at the beginning of the 20th century, my sister, wife, children and their partners agreed that it would be a great solution to bring her to the house we were renovating. With this in mind, we built my mother a bedroom, living room, bathroom and a small kitchen – the latter proving to be quite unnecessary. These lodgings were part of the house, but a door and a long corridor meant Krisia was able to have her privacy and her own routine; however, we would be nearby, being alert to any health problems and keeping her company.

Importantly, as we were aware of her aversion to change, we replicated the details of the rooms she was used to in her apartment, the same furniture, bed, photos, pictures and, of course, the television. Even Dolly immediately felt at home, despite the pack of dogs in our garden, so much so that one day, when she came to visit with my sister, it was simply a question of not taking her back to her previous address. It was a simple, non-traumatic transition, perhaps the easiest of her life.

When all this is taken into consideration, it is less complicated to imagine what was going through the mind of that young girl who had been rediscovered in a hospital in the northern regions of the world. Fear of the new. An undefined terror of change that struck at a time when her health, at least, was becoming more stable.

This too will appear vague. The time, the conversations and the decisions. From what I know, Tovek, a solitary man who worked sporadically, did not consider himself able to care for his convalescing niece. Perhaps he sent a telegram to his sister, Antonina, who had a prosperous life in Brazil, having prudently escaped Poland early on and who had lived in other countries, including India. But it is more likely he sent a letter, as this was the most common means of communication in the 1940s. I never received information on this matter. I cannot say where my mother's other uncles were located or whether any of them were consulted on this matter. I know nothing, therefore, of what happened so long ago.

I am hesitant to picture the possibility that it was a grim game of push and shove. Normal people with normal lives are not typically enthusiastic about welcoming a long lost relative into their homes (at least they were not at that time), a relative who may have picked up all sorts of habits in the filth of the ghetto and the concentration camps. I am going to shrug off this speculation and look to the immensely good side that involved my aunt (whom I always called, and she always was, my dear grandmother, in the absence of my grandmother, who had died in the war). And perhaps, more than her, to the extraordinary good will of my grandfather (also adopted by me as such and also greatly loved), Alfredo, who was a successful architect in Sao Paulo. Alfredo was a kind, polite person. I remember that when speaking to a person who deserved his respect, even by telephone, he would fasten the top button of his shirt.

Alfredo, who was not a blood relative of my mother's, was the bridegroom in the carriage, at the wedding in Krakow that had had such an effect on Krisia when she was a child. Had he not been the man he was, he could easily have changed his niece's destiny. He could have denied her shelter, almost ten years after he had seen her last.

In this strange world of bad people who commit ethnic, racial and religious persecution, some people do stand out for their altruistic attitudes. In my opinion, Grandad Alfredo, an award-winning student at the Jagiellonian University in Krakow, one of the oldest in Europe, belonged to this group of heroes. Maybe this is why, forgive me for the non sequitur, he was granted the gift of dying much later, dancing with his wife in an aristocratic hotel in the Swiss Alps, smiling of course.

When asked what day she disembarked in Brazil after the war, Krisia had the answer on the tip of her tongue: 12 May 1946. The start of a new life is indeed a memorable day. But there was another reason this date never left her memory. Every year, for the rest of his life – for the 22 years after his niece's disembarkation – Alfredo, an extraordinary man, always demonstrated his affection for my mother by ensuring that she received a dozen white roses on 12 May.

Back to the nebulous paths taken by my Polish mother from far-off Sweden to unknown Brazil: I know that by some diligent and justifiable means, Krisia's future parents managed to get in touch with a Swedish family who, in exchange for money of course, agreed to take my mother out of the sanatorium and introduce her back into a normal family, also re-teaching her basic social skills. The family thus became part of the complicated transition.

The children in the house, who were younger than my mother, magically transported her back to the childhood from which she had been ripped with the violence of dental forceps pulling out rotten teeth. I do not know the name of the family, I do not know what its line of work was, but I can easily picture all of the members being blond with translucid blue eyes. On the few occasions I heard my mother refer to this time in her life, I had the feeling she did so affectionately. There is no better proof.

Connecting with faceless people, houses with no facades, and vague timescales is a difficult task for someone who has chosen to investigate, intending to put together a story. Nobody can give me any details. I do not know whether I am writing about winter or summer, which makes a huge difference when the backdrop is Scandinavia. Nobody can tell me whether there was a town square nearby or whether it was Krisia's responsibility to take the children to school. Sometimes this may make the text monotonous, like the landscape of the plains.

I do not imagine the Swedish people were shallow. They were paid for what they did, but clearly nobody is obliged to look after a child without receiving something in return. Moreover, the supposed cold-heartedness of the Nordic people is just a silly extrapolation of the local temperature, one of those sayings that need to be forgotten. Who knows? Maybe they liked singing. In which case, the former prisoner's contribution would have been small and out of tune. Maybe they liked to do jigsaw puzzles, as they spent most of the year inside the house. It is possible, but I never saw my mother putting pieces together to make up a picture. Or maybe they enjoyed evenings drinking *Acquavit*, like so many of those who live in freezing cold places. I wonder.

Krisia was extremely young, so I am sure she did not drink any kind of alcohol at that time. She only started to drink alcohol, which she enjoyed with great parsimony, many years later. People who consume *Acquavit* sometimes get drunk and start talking nonsense. In the unlikely event of this having happened, nothing could have been said in the Stockholm residence (where her provisional caregivers lived) that would have offended her, as she had already witnessed the worst aspects of human behaviour during the war.

5

THE VULNERABLE CAPITAL

Anyone who saw *Schindler's List*, Steven Spielberg's award-winning film, based on the book *Schindler's Ark* by the Australian writer Thomas Keneally, will recall the immense wickedness with which some people treated others in that arena of the war. This is well known. However, in that film, my mother was like a stray red dot in the midst of the brutality depicted in the black-and-white footage. The concentration camp portrayed in that story is Plaszow (pronounced Puáchuv), built in 1941 on the outskirts of Krakow. The Germans constructed this place to transfer some of the multitudes of people who were then confined in the ghetto in Krakow. Tension, epidemics and violence had started to become a serious problem.

It is curious that I would surely never have known of the Plaszow's existence if it were not for the Spielberg film. My mother did not mention it on that single night of my childhood, or if she did, it was a fleeting comment that neither my sister nor I recall. I did not even know that she had ever returned to the city in which she was born. Fixed in the memory of that eight-year-old girl was the moment her father, a lawyer turned major, was separated from the family, consisting only of her and her mother.

This harrowing story of an optimistic man leaving his wife and young daughter occurred in Warsaw, the capital of Poland, more than 300 kilometres north of the city where they lived. Krisia told us that her father had the best intentions. With the imminence of the Nazi invasion, he thought it would be sensible to take his loved ones to a larger city, which would probably be better protected than would the smaller, pretty town of Krakow on the banks of the Vistula River.

It was a disastrous, well-meaning mistake. It is extremely easy to identify errors decades later, but it is likely that my grandfather's decision made complete sense at the time. Judging by the fierce antisemitism delivered in the dense spittle of Hitler and his commanders' speeches, it would have been more than fair to assume that the infantry of the Nazi army was about to advance on Krakow. It was the second largest city in Poland and had by far the largest Jewish population. In September 1939, the time of the German invasion, Krakow had 251,000 inhabitants, and 65,000 of them (a total of over 25%) were Jewish.

In the biography by Bernard Lecomte, Pope John Paul II himself, who was raised in the city and later became Cardinal-Archbishop there, recounts that almost half the pupils in the classrooms in which he studied were of the good relations between ethnic groups and religions was one of the driving forces in the city before the Second World War.

Krakow was already a cosmopolitan city in the 13th century, when it was officially founded (although records indicate that it already existed in the tenth century). It was an important commercial centre and was the capital of Poland for three long periods. The Wawel Royal Castle on the banks of the Vistula River, much visited even today, was home to several dynasties of kings.

On two occasions, it also gained a rather unwelcome place on the international stage with the invasions it suffered from neighbouring Austria.

Mainly in the 15th and 16th centuries, during the reign of the Jagiellonian kings (known to be illustrious and liberal), Jewish people who were being persecuted in other parts of Eastern Europe converged on Krakow and prospered there through activities in a number of areas. My grandfathers were born in the city. Teodor, my mother's father, and Alfredo, who adopted her after the conflict, both graduated from the halls of the Jagiellonian University, one of the oldest and most respected universities in Europe, Teodor as a lawyer and Alfredo as an architect.

A large part of the campus of this beautiful institution stretches into the bucolic Planty, the park that surrounds the old city centre, in the area once occupied by the walls that protected it. It is very well preserved because it is still in use, and contrary to what Krisia's father had imagined, Krakow remained almost unscathed during the Nazi occupation.

The artistic heritage suffered most with the arrival of the Soviet army (and the Nazis' consequent flight). It was extensively pillaged by the retreating Germans at the beginning of January 1945.

It is worth nothing that, from the end of 1940 to the beginning 1941, almost 50,000 of the city's Jewish population ceased to exist, either because they had escaped to other regions or because they had been taken prisoner or murdered. Few returned at the end of the war, and those who did changed their identities and abandoned any links with Judaism, as religion – whichever religion – was not held in high regard by the Communist regime that controlled the city until 1989.

When I was in Krakow to do reporting, almost 50 years after the end of the Second World War, several sources informed me that the local Jewish population was virtually non-existent at that time. It was, however, interesting to discover that nowadays the former Jewish neighbourhood of Kazimierz is an important tourist attraction in the city, with numerous restaurants (excellent ones, by the way) serving the typical cuisine of people who no longer live there.

Entertainment was provided in all of these restaurants by bands playing klezmer music, a non-religious Jewish genre developed by the Ashkenazim in the 15th century.

Klezmer music is sometimes heavy with pain and sometimes radiantly joyful. According to my guides, the musicians were all from Krakow and had no ties with the so-called chosen people. I talked to several of the musicians, and initially, almost all confirmed their Slavic origins, authentic Poles. When I dug a little deeper though, several of them admitted to their Jewish origins as the descendants of the few local Holocaust survivors.

I return now to the mistake (which now seems less startling) my grandfather made: In just a few days, Warsaw was occupied. In a few months, it was torn apart by the walls of the infamous ghetto. By the end of the war, it was to be the capital city involved in the conflict and that suffered the greatest destruction. Krakow, meanwhile, was almost untouched from an architectural point of view. When I visited both cities, I saw Warsaw as rows of simple uninspiring communist buildings, interlaced here and there with grandiose edifices erected to honour the Soviet civilization, responsible for shaking off the yoke of the Nazis, whereas Krakow, with its immense central square (*Rynek Glowny*), seemed to belong to a different country. Justice, however, reigns. Jewish people from both these cities and from many others throughout Poland and across Eastern Europe were treated the same and met with the same fate.

My mother said, in her youthful concept of time, that the two fugitives had enjoyed just a few days of peace in the capital. They were soon terrorized with beatings and verbal aggression, at the hands of the violent invaders, who never distinguished between adults and children. Everyone was treated as an enemy. They were ordered to shut up if they did not want to become pools of blood on the ground. Somehow, Krisia, her mother and a collection of other relatives hid for a time in a cramped basement in the Polish capital.

Once again there is a huge gap in the story, which I will fill with some of the fragments I heard over the years.

First, it should be noted that the history of Hitler, Nazism, antisemitism and the war depicts the so-called Jewish issue as being initially of secondary importance. The priority was to confine the inferior race to send them away at a later time. Some people say that the crazy Austrian corporal, turned German chancellor, considered the captivity of the Jewish people to be a tremendous punishment. While they were still alive, he said, they could be trampled on, vilified and humiliated, eventually to be killed. If they were exterminated, however, as was introduced systematically in later years, the supposed enemies of National Socialism would not provide their executors with the pleasure of seeing them bleeding slowly, the joy of hearing them plead for their lives or the almost sexual delight in subjugating them, unencumbered by any rules.

The previous paragraph was written purely to moisten the remaining hatred that has dried up in the bottom of the vessel of former generations, and though it is short, I hope it has the effect of hydrating this content. A little rage in liquid form can be a very effective defence, which apparently most of the victims of Nazism did not have.

I am putting a dose of anger in the glass next to my computer, and I will draw on it to continue this lacuna-filled narrative, which is what I have set out to do. It is fundamental that I do this because the lacunas were certainly not joyful lapses in the lives of the women. It is likely that the worst part of the story was left untold.

I made an unexpected discovery by putting together the fragments that I heard on other occasions. Teodor, the major and lawyer who left for the frontline of a war that had been lost before it started, managed to survive and return to Warsaw. He had been forced to head for the East by the rapid advance of the German forces. Sixteen days after the Nazi invasion, the Soviet army occupied his half of the crushed Polish nation, as agreed in the Molotov-Ribbentrop Pact. This was a shameless accord signed less than a month earlier, in which Communists and Nazis agreed not to enter into any dispute or fight.

On one occasion, while en route to the border with the former Soviet territory, the major was unable to escape. His horse was taken by the Red Army and he, along with other Polish military personnel with no command or purpose, was taken prisoner. My hypothesis is that the prison was close to Krakow because our fragmented family legend claims that Teodor had run the prison unit at some time in the past. Because of this, along with the inattention of the guards, he was easily able to escape captivity by means of a passage which the new owners did not know about.

It is fair to assume that Krisia, her mother and the other family members must have been hiding in the basement when Teodor returned to find his family in Warsaw, managing to dodge Germans and Russians on the way.

6

A SERIES OF PRISONS

Again, scarce information will impoverish my account of the order in which things happened. I am unable to say whether Teodor's return to Krakow was a furtive journey or whether he had connections that made it easier. It was probably not an ordeal, as I never heard any mention of this leg of the journey. Presumably the ethnicity of the group walking together could not be identified. Perhaps people were not wearing the armbands that were allotted to those who were in some way related to Abraham. The use of this identification was mandated in November 1939, but the date of this journey is unknown. Krisia, however, clarified some aspects of her own situation at this time in the recording she made for the Shoah Foundation.

My mother's interview for the Shoah Foundation is in the same indifferent style with which she always approached the subject. The lack of detail, abundant in other people's accounts, is an indication that she viewed the fact that her childhood was cut short as a trivial occurrence.

She recounts (neither looking into the camera nor avoiding it) that, when she returned to her hometown, she was taken to a nearby village where her grandfather, an industrialist with financial assets, as we will later see, had a small manufacturing unit. Krisia, along with her mother and father, went to live in a simple little house close to the factory, and she soon made friends with the local children. She wore boots, did not wash and even got dirty on purpose so as not to stand out from the others. She was accepted, played, got muddy, and for a time, she felt the sensation of being a child again. We do not know how long this innocence lasted, nor do we know the name of the place she stayed, but one day the little girl's playmates started to cast hostile glances at her. It was not long before this hostility developed into painful attacks with stones, accompanied by name calling such as "dirty Jew" and other more unpleasant terms.

The situation did not continue for long, as the Perlbergers grew scared and decided to return to Krakow. In the capital of the province Malopolska (which means little Poland), antisemitism had spread at the speed the Nazis desired.

I do not know which year I am referring to because, again, the calendar has been smudged by the dampness of time. In the interview, Krisia associates the end of her time in the village as being chronologically close to the family's move to the ghetto in Krakow. Formally, at least, the ghetto was set up on 3 March 1941, in the district of Podgórze, close to the former Jewish neighbourhood of Kazimierz.

The choice of location had to comply with technical requirements such as easy confinement and low building costs, high walls and entry points. In this particular case, the neighbourhood allocated to the Jewish people had 30 roads, 320 residential buildings and 3,167 rooms. Each apartment was split up to house four families. Wealthier families occupied larger areas. The poorest people had to make do with living on the streets.

The word ghetto is Italian in origin. As though to prove that even the greatest beauty and the most spontaneous resilience can generate spurious by-products, the expression – and the concept of confining minorities in tiny spaces – originated from Venice, in the *sestiere* (neighbourhood) of Canareggio. This famous municipality in the middle of the sea was actually born of the persecution that led fugitives to build houses on wooden poles in a small lake in the Adriatic Sea, on 117 small islands which are still as charming today.

Originally the word ghetto is a corruption of *gheto*, that means foundry in the Venetian language, because there was one in Canareggio. The despicable concept spread historically into a great number of so-called civilised countries, affecting minorities of different origins, beliefs and ideological currents.

Krisia's story contains patchy memories of her time in the ghetto. She remembers people crying, praying, singing and even an unlikely open-air wedding, in accordance with Jewish principles, held under the shade of a *chuppáh* — a kind of tent that is open on all four sides, the function of which is to protect and bless the bride and groom. She recalls too that her father, now wearing the obligatory yellow armband, wore a cape when he went out, which was usually through one of the four entry gates to the so-called Aryan world. My mother never found out what he did in the city nor how this simple trick hoodwinked the guards. The fact is that, like many other places of this nature, the ghetto in Krakow had its rebellions and attacks.

Like the one in Warsaw, it was abolished, costing thousands of lives. History tells that when it ceased to exist, it was decided that 8,000 Jewish people who were able to work would be transferred to the new concentration camp at Plászow nearby. Five thousand people were transferred to Auschwitz, where they were exterminated. Two thousand, however, died on the streets of the Podgórze neighbourhood.

I always thought that my grandfather must have been one of them because my mother's recollections of him ceased at this point. She was taken with her mother to Plaszów.

7

THE LAND OF THE DEAD

The neighbourhood of Plaszów with its hills and woodland was the location of several of the city's cemeteries. For the purposes of irony, entertainment or perhaps by chance, the Nazi leaders in Poland decided to set up a concentration camp right on land previously occupied by burial grounds.

They initially chose the areas occupied by two Jewish sacred grounds; one of these was called New Cemetery at that time. As we know, it was soon to be replaced with a much newer one built on upturned earth and overturned tombstones.

The 81-hectare area, destined for the people leaving the ghetto in Krakow, was completely closed off and began to receive inmates in October 1942. Subsequent studies estimate that, in the two years of its existence, Plaszów held a maximum of 25,000 prisoners and a minimum of 12,000.

The complex was separated from the free world by a four-kilometre-long electric fence and 12 lookout posts.

It was designed to be a labour camp for prisoners but turned into a KL concentration camp (*Konzentrationslager),* just another of the 1,200 camps built by Nazi Germany on its own territory and principally on annexed areas of land. It had the same technical rigour and inhumanity as almost all the others. For example, the 80-square-metre huts were each designed to hold 150 prisoners. And they did, although it is hard to imagine how.

There are speculations that this was actually one of the most severe and cruellest camps in the whole of paraphernalia of the Nazi prison system and not just because it was built on an area that had always been intended for the dead. *SS-Hauptsturmführer* Amon Leopold Göth, the camp commander, was responsible for making this place the epitome of evil. More details about this man appear later in this story. He was such a despicable person that, according to many accounts, he was unable to eat breakfast before he had executed at least one Jew.

Killing was, of course, one of the daily activities of the head of a concentration camp. Supposedly, however, taking pleasure in killing was an option and one Goeth embraced enthusiastically. During his administration, for example, the Great Dane, Rolf, and the German Shepherd, Ralf (both mascots of his), fed on the blood of terrified prisoners. Whenever anyone attempted to escape from the camp – an almost impossible mission at Plaszów – Goeth would retaliate by shooting ten inmates.

Although it was not an extermination camp, it is estimated that between 8,000 and 10,000 prisoners were executed under Goeth's command in an adjacent area called Hojowa Gorka, which means Penis Hill (in fact in Polish it is a rather more vulgar term for the male sex organ).

On this infamous slope, the people whom Goeth and his friends had selected were stripped, shot and buried. One of the commander's favourite guards, a German woman, Alice

Orlowski, who took great pleasure in whipping children and elderly people, was an eminent recruiter of candidates for extermination. The few people who survived Plaszów gave accounts of her brutality. However, in spite of this, Orlowski spent less than a decade of her life in prison and, like so many others, went nearly unpunished.

Relatively recent calculations show that this camp had a greater percentage of women and children than the average in other detention centres. It was also a prison where corruption was more prevalent than normal due to Goeth's venality.

Food, as in other concentration camps, was scarce and of very poor quality. Prisoners who had money, however, were able to buy supplementary rations. Profits from this business, of course, went into the commander's private coffers.

Daily life in the camp mostly consisted of stepping on tombstones, fleeing the aggressions of the commander and being beaten by the guards.

Healthy people worked in quarries and in factories making weapons and utensils intended for military use in the surrounding areas. Oskar Schindler's factory, another protagonist in this account, was one of them.

Amon Goeth ran his morbid amusement park until September 1944, when the Germans decided to transfer the remaining prisoners to Auschwitz, about 55 kilometres from Plaszów. The camp continued under the management of Arnold Büscher for a further three months.

It was during Goeth's command that the decision was taken to exhume the bodies buried at Hujowa Gorka and to cremate the mortal remains to remove any traces of the mass murders committed there. At the beginning of 1944, tractors carried out this work. According to witnesses, the operation resulted in 17 lorry loads of human ashes. The dust was spread across the region which was once again fulfilling its vocation as holy ground.

Out of all the souls who were at the Krakow prison camp, records show only 2,000 survived, the 1,200 people who were saved by Schindler's famous list plus another 800 people. My mother was in the smaller, latter group.

Plaszów stayed in the shadows for decades, just another one of the many centres for detention, torture and death in the civil hecatomb underlying the military war.

Even I had no idea how important this name had been in my mother's life, and when Thomas Keneally's book, in which he mentions it, was published, it did not spark my interest. As I recall, I considered it to be just "another testimony among so many produced after the war".

However, the book had an enormous effect on reticent Krisia who was an avid reader. She rediscovered her life in a literary concentration camp. Her fury was unprecedented. In some strange way, it reconnected her to fuses that had been passive for decades, erasing and numbing her memories. Uncommonly, she even answered back to her husband who, alarmed by the resurrection of the giant dragon of suffering, asked her to calm down.

I remember some unusual moments at this time. From one day to the next, the woman who used to talk so little underwent remarkable changes. For the first time in many years of depending physically on my father (to whom she dedicated the best of what she had to give), Krisia decided to go away for a few days, with no serious consequences. As my sister was focussed on bringing up her four small children at the time and I was at the peak of my professional life, she invited my wife to go on this unexpected journey.

They travelled to New York together. Tovek was no longer there (but he was an important part of her story), and from there they went to Washington, DC. After decades of no contact at all with her dark past, she decided to visit the recently opened US Holocaust Memorial Museum in the city. At the time it was a new incisive archive of the chronicle of the Jewish people during the Second World War.

I went there some years later and cried unreservedly at what I saw and what I imagined must have gone through Krisia's head on that visit. The museum, as though the cruelty of war was not enough, was conceived by people who were professional experts in manipulating human emotions. Visitors never leave the museum unmoved. Any person, whether or not they had any connection to the war, leaves it suffocated by the pain. I pondered that even the Nazi leaders would have done things differently had they been faced with the sensitivity of the Washington museum.

So I take another mouthful of necessary rage before some inappropriate compassion works its way into my narrative.

On her return to Brazil, her story took another turn. The fire ignited by the book and film abated, but it did not go out, nor did it remain alight as symbolic flames. Krisia never went back to being as quiet as before, but she did not make it a habit to constantly bring up her worst memories.

As mentioned earlier in this story, other survivors of the war, neither better nor worse because of it, never managed to keep quiet. Any phrase proffered by anyone they spoke to would always send them back into the deep corners of dark memories. Thus, a comment on the weather would lead to sentences such as these: "It was on a day just like this that I took my first beating." A remark about the flavour of the food being served up would invariably lead to reflections on the absence of food in the concentration camp and the wonderful taste of even a filthy piece of potato peel found on the ground, after the zombies had stepped on it repeatedly, failing to notice the value of the delicacy they had dropped.

8

SCHINDLER

Krisia opted for an unexpected middle-of-the-road approach. The subject became part of her life again, like any other part of it. When she saw the film, which came to Brazil around 1995, the realism of the set depicting Plaszów had a significant effect on her. She remembered the high walls that formed a kind of natural rampart, the shacks where she lived in conditions everyone is now familiar with and the rigour of the daily call-up to ensure that nobody had escaped, and she clearly remembered the house on high ground where the camp commander lived, SS-Hauptsturm-führer (captain) Amon Leopold Göth. He was Austrian by nationality and sick by nature, which was made worse by alcoholism and other psychoses that we need not go into here. Göth (or Goeth, without the accent) became known for his habits, which were beyond any kind of madness. The scenes watched by spectators the world over, as they sat perplexed in their cinema seats or in armchairs in front of their television sets, were not the result of fiction. Goeth really did enjoy taking his Karabiner G-43 (Gewher 43) and shooting erratically into crowds of prisoners clustered a few metres below his balcony. Obviously, the shots meant the death or serious injury of people who were only there because the Nazi leaders had not yet decided what to do with them. Cruel acts of this kind, which were without motive and went unpunished, were possible because of the aforementioned policy of the Final Solution, which had not yet been defined but that set out criteria for the extermination of all the Jewish people who had been taken captive. Another factor was the virulent antisemitism fostered by soldiers of all ranks.

Presumably Goeth was fed up with his routine as tormentor and maybe power, alcohol and the women provided by Oskar Schindler were no longer enough for him. Schindler was a German who was interested in using the free labour of the Jewish people at Plaszów to increase profit from his manufacturing contracts and the sale of tools that were fundamental to the Third Reich.

It cannot be denied that with this activity, Schindler ended up saving more than 1,000 people from Goeth's random shots and from the mass murders that followed. Liam Neeson played this character in the Spielberg film. We will return to this portrayal later, again through the lens of Krisia's memory. Its participation in the events that would be decisive in the future of the girl and her mother had such an influence on her that it provoked unexpected and aggressive discussions in the future. Of course, I will clarify later – and I am sure readers and Schindler's descendants will be shocked.

Firstly, however, we must return to a situation not registered in the books and films, being of little importance in the grand scheme of things, but which is poignant in this personal biography.

For some unknown reason, Krisia and another detainee were chosen by Goeth's baton (carried around for random beatings) to work as assistant slaves in the house on high from which this monstrous man fired shots into the surrounding area.

I listened in horror to every word my mother told me on this subject. She spoke with a level of objectivity that is only possible when telling the truth. She told me that the two girls were responsible for carrying out domestic chores and fetching and carrying. Although she must have been bedraggled and suffering from the rigours of life in the camp, Krisia was already 12 years old at this point in the war. In retrospect, I have wondered whether that lunatic also harboured sexual intentions with his choice of two girls. Of all his illnesses, lust would not even have been the most serious perversion. (But wait, I need more anger to moisten the indifference with which I came to this rational conclusion.)

My mother did not bother to go into the matter. She answered with a resounding no and told me that the captain asked them to tidy the kitchen, sweep the bedroom and fetch drink from the underground cellar, among other tasks that millions of people still do, every day, with dignity. It is their work.

But there are some elements that distinguished the work Goeth's housekeepers did from that of domestic workers of other times. The absence of payment was not a problem. It was implicit in the condition of being a prisoner that work would not be paid. In fact, it was even a privilege under those circumstances as, at least to some extent, useful people were not killed without good reason.

Krisia recalled that the hard part was the fear and, even worse than that, the terror of seeing those random shootings up close. She also remembered his aggressive, deranged yelling and erratic mood changes that led to stinging lashes to the prisoners' weak bodies. A single flash of fury could have led to the girls' deaths.

There were, of course, plenty of girls to replace them.

My grandmother was always terrified by her daughter's alarming proximity to the monster and awaited her return to their hut, internally celebrating one more day of survival. She told her daughter to take every precaution. "Be careful with the bottles! Handle them carefully! Never drop one in his presence! Always stay quiet!" she ordered. Little did she know that she was inculcating a long-lasting silence in the soul of her daughter, who was to go on to survive.

Once more I apologise for the vague facts. How long did my mother work like this – days, weeks, months or more?

On the basis of other information I gleaned from her at the end of the 20th century, I guess this torment did not last very long.

Maybe Goeth grew weary of his helpers, although this seems unlikely to me. Were this the case, they would not have had the pleasure of returning to being normal prisoners, worrying only about the shower of bullets that periodically spattered blood across the dust, or snow, in Plászow.

Poor workmanship would certainly have led to their deaths. It may be that the criminal's routine changed somehow. Maybe Krisia (I know nothing of the other girl) fell sick with one of the many infectious diseases that plagued the concentration camps, and thus Goeth, worried about being contaminated, let her go.

I know that around this time my mother suffered from whooping cough. This disease made her extremely tired. Goeth's house, as I mentioned, was situated on a hill. To reach it, she had to climb a long set of steps made from marble slabs from the cemetery that had previously existed on the site. She related that she often had to lean on the tombstones while she caught her breath in order to climb the next steps.

This may or may not be true, but fiction belongs to the world of novels. I have been tempted to romanticize this narrative on several occasions. Maybe that would make it more palatable or more unusual. Somehow though I feel that by adding colour or simply omitting facts – embedded in fact with huge doses of her and my imagination – would be an unacceptable disloyalty. After all, despite its similarity with so many other stories, this one has never been told in full, the way it deserves to be.

So we continue with the memories of the concentration camp recovered by Keneally and Spielberg, although neither ever heard my mother's story (at least not before finishing their works).

As we know, the protagonist of both pieces of art was called Oskar Schindler. The sad march at the end of Spielberg's film is a recognition of his contribution. In this scene, which is real, we see dozens of survivors walking among the tombstones of a cemetery in Jerusalem and in his honour placing a stone on his grave in the Jewish tradition. There is no other member of Hitler's party resting in any Israeli cemetery. This simple fact speaks volumes for how grateful some people were for the participation of this man, born in Zwittau (a Sudeten enclave) in the former Czechoslovakia.

Schindler's recognition of the State of Israel as "righteous among the nations" is a testament to the fact that he was actually a good man. Engraved on the auditory memories of those who saw the film is Itzhak Perlman's violin solo, a disturbing piece of music John Williams composed that plays in the background during the film's final scenes.

I have more to say (not so much) about this hero and will do so, later, once I have told the story of my mother in Plászow along with the cat.

9

THE ROLY-POLY CAT

But first the story of the roly-poly cat. It was featured in the story that Krisia used to tell her children when they were small and was revived in the recording made by the film-maker himself for the Shoah Foundation, subsequent to the movie.

A chubby cat. They often are. The moggy of this story, of no particular breed, had the peculiarity of being a plump, thriving animal that lived among starving, skeletal people.

Poor feline, it was not his fault. He was given food, cat food or whatever, and he ate it up. Any pet would do the same.

The presence of the cat, or rather, a clowder of cats, in the concentration camp was not by chance. The moggies were the family of one of the concentration camp guards who was just as obese as the animal who is joining this story now. Fiction demands that she, the guard have a name, as her real one has disappeared into the past. Margo will do. I have, however, known many women of the same name who were lovely people. I plucked this name from out of the blue.

Margo watched over, was in charge of and mistreated the detainees in the hut where Krisia and dozens of other women existed. She was strong enough to beat any captives who behaved badly, sobbed too loudly or fought over a piece of bread. She also lacked human sentiment. She was cut from the same cloth as Goeth was, the boss whose boots she licked.

However, one point in her favour was her special affection for cats, whom she referred to as "my children" and on whom she bestowed the affectionate onomatopoeia, something like *mitsimitsi*. A sweet-natured guardian as you can see.

It so happened that once a week Margo had a day off and would leave the camp to see her family, boyfriend or whatever. And so it was that my mother was chosen for another dangerous mission. She was put in charge of taking care of the felines during the woman's weekly outing. In effect this meant feeding them and watching to make sure none of them escaped. It is well known that cats are animals that have minds of their own. They are elusive, skittish and very agile. It is often said that they are much more attached to the place they live than to the people who pamper them. I have heard a number of astonishing stories of cats that were transported far away when the families they lived with moved houses and, goodness knows how, returned to the home they had left behind, despite the complicated journeys.

This phenomenon is attributed to a combination of their visual and olfactory memories, and there are many cases of moggies who spend months (even years) far from what they are convinced is their home but end up returning.

On one of the days Krisia was in charge of the creatures, the fattest one decided to run away. In a blink of the eye, presumably it climbed onto the roof of the hut and set off into the world, exercising the freedom that was never permitted to the other inhabitants at Plaszów. Cats walk when they want to, run if they feel like it, climb trees and walls and easily avoid possible predators on the way.

My mother soon realised that the chubby moggy was missing. She quickly searched all the places she was able to reach, but she could not find it. Clearly she was distraught with fear and shared her misery with her mother who told the other prisoners in the hope that the greater the number of vigilant eyes, the greater the chance of finding the fugitive.

When Margo returned from who knows where, she immediately noticed that her roundest mascot was missing. With the limitless authority bestowed on her by Adolf Hitler, she started yelling at the little carer and gave her a beating that made those looking on moan in pain. Being, however, a merciful woman, she announced loud and clear that she would give the child, who was swollen from the blows, a generous 24 hours to return the animal that had disappeared. Twenty-four hours and not a minute longer. If the feline did not return to the bosom of its zealous owner by the deadline, Krisia would be killed. Not that the death of the prisoner would make up for the absence of the fugitive, but it would make an unmistakable example of her. By murdering the lax carer, future substitutes would be fully aware of what would happen to them in a similar situation.

Obviously, the area that prisoners in a concentration camp are able to reach is limited by their condition. As important as Krisia's life was, none of them could risk overstepping the restricted boundaries set by the prison's norms. Even so, according to her testimonial, on that night, an army of prisoners (dozens, hundreds, who knows?) left their rooms to search for the fat cat. This was only possible because Margo allowed it, and the other guards in nearby huts felt sorry for her, although they probably threatened to tell Goeth if anything went wrong.

There was no disturbance to the usual order, except a multitude of prisoners whispering the cat's name the whole night long. Sadly the cat must have been busy, perhaps with another cat on heat, or maybe it had found food somewhere, but it was nowhere to be seen.

Early the following day, before the obligatory roll call, many of the inhabitants of Plaszów saw, terrified, that instead of helping look for the fat cat, Margo had been dedicating her time to building a gallows from the wood that people of her rank had access to. It was small, but big enough to rip apart the irresponsible girl's cervical vertebrae.

Faced with the prospect of meeting the end of her life at nightfall, my mother and her mother spent the day in tears. They did not pray, because as I have said, they were not religious, but other prisoners who had more faith in God did so on their behalf.

Death is part of the daily life of people imprisoned in any concentration camp. Along with being the target of stray bullets fired by Amon Leopold Goeth, people died of starvation and a wide range of illnesses, and some even took their own lives when the rare opportunity arose. But to die because a cat had disappeared, and may reappear at any time, was the most abject of reasons.

There is no suspense in this ludicrous story that occurred such a short time ago if we think in terms of the history of humankind. The fact that I am sitting at this keyboard, perfectly able to tell the tale, is proof that Margo's gallows were not used that evening. Again, I would like to know the time of year this happened, to imagine the colours and other aspects of the day on which my mother did not die.

If anybody assumed that Margo was overcome by an act of mercy, I am afraid they were optimistically deceived. At some time during the day, the roly-poly cat rejoined the other cats, with the innocence of irrational beings. I do not know who was the first to witness the miraculous return that echoed in sighs of relief around those who had been involved in the collective suffering. I know that Margo took her mascot onto her lap, mumbling something. And Krisia was never given that task again. She was forgotten. The little gallows must have been thrown on the scrap heap.

10

FAMILY TIES

As this narrative is replete with comings and goings, I cannot say whether the incident of the roly-poly cat was before or after Oskar Schindler's participation in my mother's story. I should like to make it clear that despite my interest in the matter, I had never heard the name of the Sudeten industrialist before the publication of the book that led to the film, both of which were the cause of bad memories, great resentment and, of course, considerable uncertainty. It is known that Schindler saved around 1,200 Jewish people by making them his private property in a way. This happened just before the implementation of the so-called Final Solution, the best extermination plan that Nazi power could have carried out.

Being a friend (fake friend) of Amon Goeth, he managed to take a large number of Plaszów detainees and place them on the production line of his kitchen utensil factory in Krakow, at number 4, Lipowa Street. These days, this address has been transformed into a tourist pilgrimage, although all that remains of it are the walls. The business, run by the Sudeten, was called Emalia and would later branch out from plates and saucepans into making capsules for artillery and grenades. According to historical records, the so-called benefactor had managed to get authorisation to build his own shacks on a piece of ground next to the factory where he housed as many as 558 in-house workers. The "employees" of the first phase of Emalia were recruited from among the prisoners according to their qualifications and the company's needs. Later, however, when the difference between being with Schindler or with Goeth was a choice between life and death, people paid what they could to be on the list.

It is known that Goeth, the demented captain, made a number of attempts to take prisoners back to the camp. These attempts were always circumvented by Schindler's sweet talk. Details about the nature of the industrialist's charms (or bewitching) are not known.

Numerous accounts from a variety of sources that have come to be accepted as true mention the possibility that Schindler earned much more money selling the freedom of enslaved Jewish people than by producing utensils with an unpaid workforce.

I am bringing up this controversy only because my mother (and my grandmother) were not on the salvation list produced by the "righteous among the nations" and his assistants. Maybe they were just unlucky. Some may believe it plausible that the list was put together randomly.

It so happens, and I was unaware of this until I started deeper investigations into the incidents I am relating here, that others, several members of the Lewkowicz family, the original lineage of both my grandmothers (my adopted one and the one who died) were in Plászow at the same time. My mother already had the surname of Perlberger, which she had inherited from the major and, by marriage, so did my grandmother Felicja, who died as she looked on as her daughter was saved by British soldiers.

The presence of relatives at the same camp and the later certainty that several of the other Lewkowicz family members were included on Schindler's list reveals horrifying possibilities.

I do not have more evidence to shed light on this, but we must go back some years in time to discover that the patriarch of the family, a certain Bernardo, had been a prosperous and great industrialist in his town before the German invasion. His large factory in Kobyerzin, originally a pottery, had become the principal manufacturer of construction materials in the province of Malopolska. This is why, despite its Jewish origin, the Lewkowicz family did not live in Kazimierz, the neighbourhood where the Jewish community lived and a neighbour of the district of Podgórze, which would later be walled up and transformed into a ghetto. The family lived instead in Kleparz, a region where only the well-to-do resided.

I heard that the business fortune that was left (once the Germans, Poles and other bloodsuckers had taken what they could) fell into the hands of family members, many of whom were in Plaszów. I do not know what became of Bernardo, whether he disappeared or died or what happened to him. Someone told me (I no longer remember who) that Bernardo's wife, Billa, who would therefore be my great-grandmother, committed suicide when she was sent to the ghetto. Once again, facts are missing from this story, which means I have to fill the gaps with suppositions or rely on my somewhat flawed memory.

The fact is that one of the seven siblings, probably the eldest, known as Fredek (whose name was Ferdynand), apparently kept the money in his care. It had been turned into gold, watches and precious stones. I do not know how much it was all worth, but it is not difficult to imagine that they had hidden it in a niche in the wall of the shack they lived in or under a floorboard.

In other words, in the absence of his parents, Fredek was in charge of their wealth. He controlled negotiations – this certainly happened – and was the guardian of any guarantee of the future life of any family members who survived.

My mother remembers seeing Fredek talking to Oskar Schindler and buying his relatives' freedom. It seems that in this way he saved one or two of his brothers who had not escaped before the war and possibly their sons, if they had any. When I looked at the list, I found the following Lewcovicz, with the exact same spelling of the family name: Ferdynand, Herrmann, Icek, Ital, Moses and Nathan. No women. Was Ferdynand a misogynist?

It is possible he only saved men or, and this is likely, he also saved some of the female relatives whose surnames had changed through marriage. There are no answers to these questions. But there are two indisputable facts: The Sudeten industrialist definitely did sell freedom (even if he did so with noble principles or because of the utmost need to keep Goeth happy), and this Fredek, who as I recall turned out to be as bad as the concentration camp commander, used money that was not his to buy people's freedom. But only the freedom of people chosen by him, thus creating a kind of abject "Fredek's List".

Some may rightly wonder how a young girl could remember events like these. The vehemence with which

Krisia did so made it impossible to doubt her account of her eldest uncle's choices, who by the way was about 35 years old at the time. It was such a traumatic incident for both her and her mother. From one moment to the next, the rest of the Lewcowicz family disappeared from the camp, through a gate that led them to Schindler's factory, and more significantly, to life. All that was left to the sister and niece abandoned in Plaszów was a sense of hopelessness and the prospect of death. It is easy to imagine the fear and indignation that led both of them to hysteria. On the other side of the gate, the two rejected women must have yelled until their relatives could no longer hear them.

This is an episode that could never be forgotten. Not even a weak little girl could get this unspeakable act on the part of her uncle out of her head.

Fifty years later I was at a dinner party with a number of others and witnessed a further episode in this story. It happened around the dining table at my parents' house in Campos do Jordão. There were always guests there because my father, more than my mother, enjoyed company. Friends and family enjoyed spending time with Sven Hein. (Now his name appears in the story. It was derived from the name of a Swedish poet and explorer called Sven Hedin, whom my grandfather Ludwig admired.) For many years, my father, who will feature again in this story, was known for his good humour, jokes and the limitless affection he displayed towards my mother, his children, grandchildren and other relatives.

On that day, my grandmother Antonina, Krisia's adopted mother who was so important to her, and some others were at the table. She was a discrete woman who spoke quietly in a strong Polish accent. If I am not mistaken, this was the only occasion on which I saw her flare up. And she really did! The topics of conversation were the usual chit chat, the cold climate in the Mantiqueira mountains, and I think we talked about the dogs that lived in the house, adored by their owners.

My mother and my grandmother started to speak in Polish, the language that had united them since they were young. This was nothing out of the ordinary, because Antonina used to get lost in Portuguese dialogues and would resort to her native tongue. So everything was perfectly normal up to this point. I recall that dessert had already been served when both of them unexpectedly raised their voices. In just a few seconds, all the other diners fell silent. Nobody had the faintest idea what they were discussing. Suddenly, Krisia and her mother started to shout in an unprecedented manner.

It still gives me the shivers when I remember both of them getting up from the table. My mother's eyes were full of a rare hatred. My grandmother, whose eyes were wide open and tearful, seemed to be defending the indefensible. Suddenly she burst into sobs, left the table still talking, and we could hear from afar the force with which she slammed the door of her bedroom shut.

We were all shocked and waited for the dust to settle before demanding subtitles to the violent discussion. A little calmer, but also in tears, unusual for my mother, she explained that, for the first time, she had accused Fredek of excluding them from salvation, with no clear motive, other than eventually avoiding having to share the remaining valuables with more people.

The brutal accusation must have hit my grandmother Antonina hard. After all, Fredek was her brother. He had graduated in medicine before the war and must have been the prodigal son of the Lewcowicz family before the curtain of terror closed on all of them, turning them into people, in this case, capable of the worst attitude imaginable.

My grandmother's eldest brother had no way of defending himself at this point. A few years after he'd reached the United States, where he intended to settle, he was the victim of a fatal car accident.

I can understand the indignation and later doubt that entered my grandmother's heart at that meal. As I write these lines, even I cannot help wondering whether there was another reason or explanation for what Fredek had done. I sincerely hope there was something that would redeem him.

Fortunately, despite the virulence everyone saw that day, my grandmother did not ask to leave the house she was staying in. Krisia never returned to the subject, and as far as I know, they continued to love each other until the end of Antonina's life, at the end of the 20th century. Proof of this was that every day I can remember they would spend hours chatting to each other on the phone (in Polish of course). There was a password for these conversations: "*Tak, Ciociu*", or "Yes, Auntie", my mother's way of starting the phone calls.

Back to that time in the past then – any hope for the two women, abandoned by their family, had disappeared. I do not know very much about what happened after this. It is possible that the incident of the roly-poly cat occurred after their separation from the family. In the books it says that once the systematic extermination of the remaining Jewish people had been decided, there was no longer any need to retain the camps, the purpose of which was concentration, a synonym for agglomeration, of prisoners.

The history books state that the concentration camp at Plaszow closed in August 1944. But there are mistakes in all the factual records of this period of the war, principally because the end of Nazism had already begun, and the previously detailed accounts by military personnel, many of whom had attended good German universities, gave way to worthless scraps of paper that gradually deteriorated as the Soviet troops moved closer on the East and Western Allied soldiers began to occupy growing areas on the west of the Thousand-Year Reich, which was clearly falling apart.

Even accounts of the death of the depraved Amon Goeth is told differently depending on the source. Some say he committed suicide when he was cornered after being discovered in Krakow, where he had fled in search of associates to conceal him.

The widely accepted version however is that immediately after being identified by North American military staff after the war, Goeth was extradited from Germany to Poland. He was imprisoned; the world takes unexpected turns as we all know, and he was put on trial by the Supreme National Court in Krakow between 27 August and 5 September 1946. The magistrates were probably Soviet lawyers under pressure from the country's new occupiers. He was accused of numerous crimes, among them torture and the indiscriminate execution of thousands of people. No longer protected, the captain was hanged, at the Montepulich prison, on 13 September of the same year. It is said that, crazy as ever, he shouted at the top of his lungs "Heil Hitler!" before hanging lifeless from the rope that bore his name. Montepulich is very close to where the Plaszów camp had been and some scant versions state that his execution took place at the very prison he had commanded. This is hard to believe, but the hypothetical execution of the criminal at the very camp at which my mother spent so much time would be poetic. And it would be even more ironic if they had had hanged Goeth from the little gallows that had once been constructed for Krisia because of a chubby cat.

It is also said that this extremely perfidious man's ashes were thrown in the River Vistula. I feel sorry for the fish that lived in its currents at that time.

I notice that the narrative here is becoming soaked in the rage I had placed in the glass by my side, some paragraphs earlier. I ask for your understanding of this momentary lack of impartiality, although I confess a formal commitment to do so was not made by this author in reliving his own mother's story.

In fact, now that this point is clear, I will not return to this subject.

11

THE BRIGHT BLUE CAMP

How do you clear out a concentration camp? Should there be a get-together, party gifts and acknowledgement on both sides that "that was not good"? However, I imagine those remaining at Plaszów being driven out by their captors.

On consulting a map of that period, I saw that there used to be a train station right in front of the camp. As has been depicted in films, photos and other records, the prisoners were probably piled up like sardines in cattle wagons. Those who still had the strength or courage to complain, although this is unlikely at that juncture, must have been shot.

No doubt some of the guards, who were soon to lose their jobs, planned some last-minute fun, wiping people out for no reason at all. Goeth would certainly not have hesitated to do such a thing.

Thousands of people died in transit to the extermination camps because they were weak, could not breathe and of course were unable to drink even a drop of water.

In the case of those leaving Plaszów, the journey to their deaths was quite a short one. It was less than 60 kilometres from Krakow to Auschwitz-Birkenau, the gigantic complex that sent a million people up in smoke. In other words, it is unlikely that anyone lost their lives on that short journey.

The scenes that are so often shown, of new inmates being welcomed by a small band of musicians close to the gate, singing "*Arbeit macht frei*" (*work sets you free*), are not from this time. The musicians in striped uniforms belong to a period in which the new arrivals still clung to the hope of continuing their sorry lives in a different place. Once the Final Solution had been decided, there was no reason for this song and dance. They knew they would eventually leave that place via the immense chimneys that spewed soot day and night.

My mother told me that it was no secret. Those who got off the train knew precisely what went on at that location. The rumours increased and were often repeated, via a sort of informal radio that existed in the world of the captives. A handful of fitter people, among them my father-in-law, André or Andor, who arrived in Birkenau at the end of the war, were sent to work in the factories that had sprung up around the camp to make use of the slave labour. Andor was 16, so he was not quite as battered as most of the others (although he was not exactly a strapping lad). He had the notorious inmate number tattooed on his right arm and went to serve in the I.G. Farben (Interessen-Gemeinschaft Farbenindustrie AG), a chemical factory, the speciality of which at that time was to produce Zyklon B, a lethal gas used to kill prisoners. The company was officially dissolved in 1952, but in practice, it continued activities under the names Agfa, BASF, Bayer and Hoechst Sanofi, several of which still feature in Brazilian industrial parks.

Andor Stern turned out to be the only survivor of Brazilian nationality held at Auschwitz-Birkenau, and we will return to his story.

Just now, we need to focus on the two small red dots I referred to before – my grandmother and my mother – being thrown from a sordid rail wagon and sent to a long queue leading to a room next to the chimney.

I have to say that when I went to Auschwitz with a group of Brazilian journalists and some young European diplomats who had no direct emotional connection with the history of the camp, I understood that there is no escape from the terror it evokes. When you are still in the film theatre adjacent to the entrance of the complex, you see again those shocking scenes of a time at which humanity reached the lowest point in its history (this may be an exaggeration, as other equally repulsive massacres happened both before and after in different parts of the world). However, the most distressing part is the accounts given by a number of people, some of them unsophisticated people who worked there years later or lived nearby. More than one person mentioned that often at night the ground in the camps shines bright blue. This comes from the earth that until today, and forever, is impregnated with tonnes of human ashes scattered there.

During the respectful guided visit, with a highly trained guide, nobody could take their eyes from the ground, made of lives taken away for no reason.

I do not think this is the time or place for me to go deeper or repeat what so many others have said about this place, which is sacred because of the lives that ended there and evil because of the terrible use it was put to. I can say though that everyone in the group with me on that day spent the afternoon in silence and at night drowned their sorrow at belonging to the same species in numerous shots of the renowned local vodka.

Schindler's so-called protégés headed in the opposite direction to Auschwitz. On 14 October 1944, a train took 700 men to Zwittau-Brinnitz, where the factory had been transferred and where it functioned until the end of the war.

The women, around 300 from the same list, boarded the train on the 21st of October. A logistical error occurred that was almost irreparable. The women, saved afterwards by the "righteous among the nations", were mistakenly placed in one of two carriages on a long train that was taking about 2,000 women to Auschwitz. Therefore, the destination was death and not the factory they had been promised.

Schindler was far away, taking care of his new factory, and it seemed the error would not be fixed.

However, as soon as he heard that "his" women were headed for the furnace at the extermination camp, Schindler managed to get some of his old Nazi friends, who had the power to revert this normally irreversible situation, to act. It is hard to say what strings were pulled or how 300 Emalia workers escaped.

In the Spielberg film, the miracle occurs when the women, already naked and their heads shaved, are in the dreaded "showers", which never emitted one drop of water, only the vapours of the lethal poison.

The story was likely exaggerated to intensify how close to death Schindler's women came. Maybe not. The fact is that from one minute to the next, they were removed from the gas chamber, given other clothes and sent back to the rail wagon, this time destined for freedom.

In any case, the fact that they had come so close to the end must have marked them for the rest of their lives, exacerbated by their belief that the Sudeten had betrayed them at the 11th hour.

Many years later, my mother told me she had been on the same train that had left Plaszów on 21 October. She did not have the ticket to salvation given (or bought) by the women on the list and on the journey; she overheard the indignation and whimpering of the group that was already cursing its absent saviour.

I am retelling these facts because something similar happened to my mother and my grandmother, who had been excluded from the list. On this point, Krisia's memory, clearly dulled by the terror of the situation, may have failed her (or not – which would make the end of this story even more heroic).

They were both sent to the extermination complex, as they had nobody to save them. The story I am writing now would not even exist if it were not for a stroke of luck that saved them. In my mother's words, they were queuing up for certain death next to some buildings with windows. These do indeed exist and are on the path to the gas chamber, but even when I looked at everything onsite and very closely 60 years later, I was not able to reconstruct the picture described by Krisia on that night during my childhood.

In her description, she and her mother, always inseparable, were walking towards their inevitable end when someone noticed a broken pane in the hinged window next to them. Looking through it, my grandmother spotted another queue of people walking in the opposite direction. The destination of the people in that queue was unknown, but at worst, it was just another path to the end, maybe longer, maybe shorter. My grandmother Felicja was very thin and managed to squeeze through the gap, pulling my mother by the arm. Neither the guards behind nor in front of them in the queue noticed their movements. The two escaped prisoners composed themselves as best they could and started to walk towards the unknown. According to my mother – she had many nightmares about this scene throughout her life – another woman tried to escape through the same window seconds later. The poor woman however was spotted by an inspector who shot her then and there and with a noise familiar to everyone.

I could not find any record of a train that left Auschwitz-Birkenau with prisoners on board in any of the sources I consulted except for the group of women who worked for Schindler. By definition, the repulsive annihilation centre was a place for arrivals, never departures. It was only later, when the enemies of the German army were drawing closer, that the Nazis hastily "relocated" the remaining prisoners in an attempt to minimize their humanitarian sins, usually forcing them to leave on foot in what became known as the death marches, the effort of which only a few skeletal humans survived. Reports exist that when it became clear the Germans' crimes against innocent civilians were about to be uncovered, even the trains were used to transport prisoners (or what was left of them) to German territory. Thousands of captives were swiftly removed from all the camps that were close to the advancing Soviet soldiers. In the circumstances, not even the voracious annihilation methods would have been enough to mitigate the Nazi guilt.

The attempt to clean things up was so obvious that it can be seen today that the chimneys were destroyed at most of the crematoriums in Birkenau so they would not provide concrete proof of the cruelty of their commanders. The tactic was partially successful.

Proof of this is that the famous Nüremberg trial, set up by the nations that won the war to try war criminals, ended in an almost unbelievable 12 people being sentenced to death. Just one dozen.

Clearly, there were other courts, in different places, that sentenced murderers (like the one that sentenced Amon Goeth to death by hanging), but the small number of people who were held accountable for their animal-like behaviour suggests that the world had decided to wipe the slate clean of the history of the Holocaust. I met survivors who would have rejoiced if all Germans had been executed (even the innocent ones) and the land of Goethe, Beethoven, Wagner and Nietzsche had been transformed into an immense unin-habited park in the middle of Europe.

I shall leave this type of deviation aside for now, as this inhabits the terrain of revenge.

I return now to the sad train station where passengers arrived and never left. I note, however, that there are further lapses in the story because I do not know how to explain what happened next.

According to my mother, the queue in which both women found themselves took them to the Bergen-Belsen concen-tration camp, in German territory in Lower Saxony, more than 1,000 kilometres from Auschwitz and certain death.

Officially at least, Bergen-Belsen was not an extermination camp. Death was not a certainty there. It was just probable, as is recorded in the many photographs of dead bodies piled up in the shape of pyramids. British soldiers later removed the bodies during the liberation of the area. The grim captivity, created for the sole purpose of "housing" prisoners of war (above all, for possible exchanges) was in Germany itself, in the province of Lower Saxony, 17 kilometres north of the town of Celle.

There were large installations . Almost all of the 50,000 prisoners who died in Bergen-Belsen fell victim to the numerous diseases that plagued the area from the end of 1944 when it became a kind of cesspool, into which thousands of Jewish prisoners, evacuated from camps situated closer to the Eastern front, were thrown, with no criteria, planning or hygiene. It is possible that this is the reason my mother and grandmother's transfer from Auschwitz to Bergen-Belsen was never registered.

The afflictions that led to the high death rate were typhoid, tuberculosis and different kinds of dysentery. According to records, the British, who liberated the camp, found around 60,000 prisoners in the camp, most of whom were either seriously ill or dying.

Thousands of prisoners died after gaining the freedom they had dreamed of. Only 12,000 people were left (20 percent of the total), and they were transferred to a nearby camp set up by the British and the Allies.

The rest formed the pyramid of bodies I spoke of earlier.

I suggest that when you look at these photographs of lifeless children, women, elderly and sick people piled up, you bear in mind that 12 people were held accountable and sentenced to death during the council that evaluated those responsible for the slaughter of innocent civilians. Twelve people, not even enough to form a football team with reserves on the bench.

It is impossible to say how long Krisia stayed at Bergen-Belsen (once again, I come up against a scarcity of information). The soldiers arrived on 15 April 1945, some days before the end of the war in Europe. The Second World War officially lasted until 2 September that year, when the Japanese finally surrendered.

For all intents and purposes, 15 April was considered to be the day on which my grandmother Felicja died. It is said, or it is a beautiful legend, that she was in hospital dying of typhoid. This disease swept through the camp, where poor Anne Frank was also held (she was killed there in February). The brave woman held tightly to the frail ties that had kept her in this world until she was certain her daughter was free. That the British were nearby was common knowledge in the final days of Bergen-Belsen's existence, but she had already lost a child. Her son, Arthur, whose faded photo is still in my mother's bedroom, had died of scarlet fever before the war. She had no intention of allowing her second child to be taken from her.

In the days before the British saviours arrived, my mother had the opportunity to visit the hut where the dying were sent in the messy detention centre, abandoned by the directing body who had already fled. People cried copiously there. She never cried.

Nobody is contaminated by this fatal illness by being near to or breathing the same air as the sick. It is a bacterial infection transmitted by mites, lice and ticks – a collection of insects that my father-in-law called one's own personal zoo. It infests installations where people are destined for certain death.

In other words, Krisia may have had typhoid, as well as tuberculosis, when the Red Cross sent her to the Swedish sanitorium. There are no records of the diseases that afflicted the people rescued from the final gasps of systematic cruelty. Felicja let go of the fragile web that had kept her alive in a world that had been hostile for so very long, when the war ended and the Germans, either dead or gone, would never be able to lay a finger on her daughter.

Two decades ago, I conducted some research in an archive on the concentration camps, in search of any text or image that could transport me back to the beginning of the European summer of 1945. I watched as the woman with access to the documents shook her head sadly. "Unfortunately," she said, "we hardly have anything on Bergen-Belsen. The British burned down the entire camp on 21 May because of the widespread infectious diseases."[1]

"All I have is this, provided by a British soldier before the end," she said as she handed me a piece of photographic paper, slightly damaged by the passage of time, about 15 cm wide and 10 cm long. It was a picture of a group of malnourished girls, sitting side by side inside a warehouse in the prison in Lower Saxony.

In the middle of them – believe me, this is not fiction or an emotional appeal – was my mother's face, an undeniable image to last for eternity. The archive woman saw my eyes misting, and without my asking, she made a copy of the old photo.

As she passed me the copy, she even apologised for not giving me the original photo. "You know, it is the only one we have in the archives," she explained. I wonder why the world is not inhabited purely by this kind of person.

If I had not been so shaken by the discovery, I would have kissed her affectionately on the forehead.

12

ANDOR'S STORY

The Second World War did not end with a simple document of surrender. It ended gradually and in stages for the victims who had survived. In many cases, as we will see later, a prisoner's return to what could be considered freedom was a long, painful process, sometimes not concluded.

Krisia went to Sweden. Andor was sent to Munich, the capital of the province, after he was removed from a wagon full of dead bodies on the train tracks alongside the Steinberger See, in Bavaria.

The two images do not match and do not complement each other. Nowadays, the lake is a popular destination for water skiers. It is one of the many natural beauty spots in the southern region of Germany, close to the Alps. The silent convoy, full of living dead (dead bodies and some barely alive), lulled by the lapping of the small waves made by the breeze on the lake of melted ice coming off the mountains, was an unexpected, horrific interference with the peacefulness of that place.

American soldiers sent Andor and his close friend Lajos to the Bavarian metropolis. This place had a strong Nazi Party base. The intention had been to create an empire that would last 1,000 years grounded on racial supremacy. Among the rubble of ideas and buildings, the survivors were sprayed with clouds of HBC in their new home to rid them of a multitude of insects picked up in captivity. They were then accommodated in a collection of tents in the midst of the debris of the city. With time, food (ah, food!) and the good-will of the soldiers, they recovered from their illnesses but became sick with worry. What could they do? How would they start over? How could they face the near certainty that the families they had lived with before they were separated must have died?

Before they found answers, the two men, now recovered, started to frequent and participate in a grim market for survivors that sprang up at that time in the city. In this ruined square, the widows of thousands of German men who had never returned, exchanged items no longer of use – shirts, trousers, shoes and so on – for potatoes, oranges and whatever else they could subsist on.

But their questions persisted: Should they return to Budapest in search of their old routines that probably no longer existed? Or, assuming that the worst had actually happened, should they go back to see if by chance they could reconnect with any survivors who had been mistakenly taken for dead? Was it worth it?

Of course, hope is stronger than fear, even when fear has already become the modus operandi. Andor and Lajos managed to return to the city they had lived in. Andor's story is told in the book *Uma luz na escuridão* (A light in the dark), written by Gabriel Davi Pierin. His account is therefore much more complete.

Approximately three months after they were freed, the boys were given safe passage and travelled to the ancient republic of the Magyar. Disappointed because they had not found anybody there, they returned to Munich in search of a certain Mr David who had promised them a place on one of the ships leaving Europe for Palestine, the promised land for those who had nowhere else to go.

Unfortunately, Mr David had already left with his refugees. The autumn was setting in. The two youths had spent the summer in their persecutors' great city, and once again, they decided to go to Budapest to make a more detailed search. It worked. The first time returned, they had not considered that other survivors from their families might take longer to make it back to their country of origin.

On the second attempt, some re-encounters occurred, but only a few. As time went by, new names were added to the list of losses. More tears were spilled. New memories were sculpted in the inner memorial of those who had survived.

Now I should explain that Andor was born in Brazil, by chance, in the neighbourhood of Bela Vista, in São Paulo. He was only registered there because his father, the doctor István Stern, had been hired by the mining company Anglo Gold Ashanti, based in Nova Lima (Minas Gerais) to assist people who were hurt in the always dangerous process of extracting metals from the earth's depths. The South African company is still active in a number of places around the world, and its speciality is gold. It has been in Brazil for almost 200 years.

Andor's mother, Julia, was pregnant with her only son at the time. She refused to brave the difficulties expected of life in the mining hinterland at that time and ended up having her son in the capital of the state of São Paulo.

The couple and their offspring moved to another of the company's installations in India soon after. The episode, however, meant Andor, André in Brazil, carried a Brazilian passport. This was forgotten in a drawer and was of no use at all when the family returned to Hungary, unintentionally exposing themselves to the perverse effects of the impending war.

Holding a passport of a nation considered an enemy of the Germans and the Hungarians under Nazi domination caused problems for the 14-year old. In yet another decision issued by the local governors, all foreign residents in the Hungarian capital were obliged to report to the authorities. A large group of people of a number of nationalities, almost all of whom were of Jewish origin, were arrested and taken to a place near the Carpathian Mountains. Under the command of violent guards, the inmates had to cut down trees to construct a building in which they would later be confined. Andor was the youngest.

A fellow prisoner, a British citizen who had some precious stones hidden in the heel of his shoe, decided to use part of his treasure to escape. He took pity on the Brazilian lad and decided to invite him to come along. The pair arrived in the Hungarian capital days later, and the young man was escorted to his grandparents' house in the suburbs. There was less risk of being reported there. But Andor's mother decided to take him back home. For a while, the boy remained in hiding there, not able to go beyond the confines of his backyard. Once it seemed likely that his escape from the Carpathian Mountains had been forgotten, he took a job at an electrical components factory that belonged to a friend of the family. Jewish interns were still being taken on by some companies, and the accidental Brazilian has happy memories of those days. Even though he wore the yellow armband that had recently been made obligatory in the country, Andor was not afraid to leave the factory and walk around the streets. He even took the Jewish identification off to reduce the risk of an unpleasant surprise when walking near the factory. "I think young people believe they are invincible. Death seems so distant that they underestimate the dangers." He said afterwards and he repeated this many times in the seminars he gave for young Brazilian students decades later.

Invincibility strengthens the spirit, but nothing to be done when the enemy decides to extinguish it. Along with all the other Hungarian Jews, Andor was put on a train headed for extermination.

Because he held the green (and yellow) passport of a far-off South American country, the young man went down in history as the only Brazilian prisoner at Auschwitz and, as chance would have it, the only survivor from the land of Getúlio Vargas. He remembers – he is alive and kicking as I write these lines – that the Nazis had to make a special uniform for him to wear, on which his nationality was identified with a capital B and a small r, perhaps the only one of its kind in the extermination centre's chronicle of horrors.

After the war, he was cared for by his surviving relatives (in particular, he remembers Aunt Elisabeth, or Bözi Neni, if that is how it is spelt), but the ex-inmate could not settle, nor could he imagine a future on the sad continent where he lived (already newly divided by the Cold War). So he asked his aunt to let him start a new life in the country where he was born. She gave him her blessing and a good deal of money – part of which he blew, without hesitation – before he boarded a ship in the city of Genoa, headed for Santos.

13

RE-CIVILISATION

After a long period in Sweden of learning about civilisation, Krisia boarded a ship with the same destination as that of Andor. The former inmate must have already had an idea of how to behave at the dining table and how to form basic human relationships, and she must have shown signs that she would be capable of starting her life again with people who had not gone through prolonged trauma, who had not been whipped or come close to death.

This is just an honest evaluation given the distance, at that time, between the world she had come from and the one for which she was headed. There is much written and filmed demonstrating the difficulty of integrating former prisoners into their close families. Their families may well not have lived through the same horror as them. It cannot be said that either party is right or wrong. Taking a compassionate stance, it is easy to put oneself in the place of the victims who survived the Holocaust. However, the position of those who, through no fault of their own, did not undergo the same ordeals, also needs to be respected. People in the reintegration phase sometimes behaved (in others' eyes) like ogres, for example, in their personal hygiene. How could a person who had been confined for six years, in the worst possible conditions, understand the rules of the game in the bathroom? Where to sit, where to wash, the priorities in the process of cleaning themselves, the purpose of soap, shampoo and toothpaste, not to mention the use of sanitary towels and hair removal creams and many other details we do not think twice about when we are free and are, at least minimally, aware of what is and is not acceptable.

All this must have been fully taught in the home of the nameless Swedish family. Every detail would have been made clear to avoid embarrassment when Krisia returned to what we could call the routine of a Western human being.

Even so, as we shall see, my mother's reintegration into a peaceful household was not so straightforward.

The Swedish family that took in the former inmate was obviously a human community with all the behavioural conditioning of the time. My mother remembered her Scandinavian guardian's concern about preparing her to go to Brazil. Not without reason, she believed that going to a remote, poor country in South America, Krisia could come up against new problems. She feared the child, already deeply scarred, would tread a thorny path.

Above all – notice how incorrigible human beings are – she feared my mother, who was almost 15 years old, may fall victim of a black man, either through sexual abuse or marriage. Racism, once again, underpinned a well-intentioned and kind concern.

I learned, from Krisia, that these warnings frightened her. All the accounts given by the Malmö host were scary and painted a picture of people of colour as being primitive, dangerous and aggressive. At that time there were no black people in Sweden, which made the people there prone to the possibility of renewed segregation policies.

By way of illustration of the turns the world can take, I recall a strange incident from my childhood. I was playing football with some friend in the driveway, next to the house where I lived until I got married, when I saw an unusual couple coming towards me. At that time, houses had flimsy, almost decorative gates not designed for security purposes. The woman had very fair hair and skin and looked beautifully seductive to me. The man at her side had very dark skin, a slightly green tone I thought, and long straight hair. I had never seen such an unusual-looking person. I went to the entrance and heard the blond woman ask me something in a language I did not understand. I gestured to her to wait and ran to find my mother. When the two women saw each other, there was a frisson of delight, and they greeted each other affectionately.

Next, Krisia invited the strangers into the lounge and asked Dona Anita, her long-standing maid, to make some coffee. They chatted for something like two hours. As I could not understand a word of what they were saying, I went back to playing ball against the wall of the house, which left marks and every now and then earned me a slap.

Later, after saying goodbye to the couple – yes, they were a couple and left holding hands – my mother told me that that pretty lady had once been her Swedish sister and that the young man, a Hindu, was her husband, to the huge dismay of her mother, jealously racist, who still lived in Malmö.

The ship that brought my mother to Europe, like nearly all at the time, was divided into three classes. At the expense of her Brazilian family, the young refugee crossed the Atlantic in the most luxurious of these and was of course delighted with the way she was treated on board. After a number of stops on the way, the transatlantic made its first Brazilian stopover in Recife.

From the deck, the refugee could see the city, which had large favelas at that time. The poverty was not unlike that of the camps she had been in. Moreover, my grandfather Alfredo, who did not want her to feel lonely, had asked a friend of his to look after her and take her on a tour of the city. It was the first time Krisia saw dark-skinned people, exactly as her guardian had described them, wearing ragged clothes that were worse than the uniforms worn by prisoners of war.

She recovered from her first impression when she reached the port of Rio de Janeiro, and new feelings overcame her when she arrived in Santos. The shy girl, arriving from Sweden, was welcomed by her aunt and uncle (my Brazilian grandparents) who spoke perfect Polish. They had a silver American car with red leather seats and a smiley driver.

As I said, this branch of the family was wealthy. Along with being an architect, my grandfather Alfredo was a partner in a construction company called Luz-Ar, a big name in São Paulo.

The warm reception filled the young refugee with hope. It had been many years since she had enjoyed joyful affection. There were also a considerable number of Polish friends of my grandparents at the port. They were curious to meet the poor little thing.

This initial pleasure did not last too long. When she got to her new home, on Alameda Jaú, she met someone who had not gone to the Santos port, being, as she certainly was, full of hatred. It was her new sister, ten-year-old Olga who had been the undisputed queen of the Düntuch family home until then (this was my grandfather's name).

From then on, Olga and Krisia – who became Krystyna in Brazil, as her original name, a Slavic diminutive, was unknown here – were never friends of any sort. They lived separately, in their own corners of the house, without any apparent affection for each other. Was Olga a bad person?

I do not think so, although her lack of affection extended to my sister, my children and me, and future family gatherings were always tinged with a frosty chill. I think it is plausible to believe that to that girl, who was also born in Poland, but had integrated into Sao Paulo society years earlier, Krystyna was always a bad-mannered intruder who she dearly wished had never come to Brazil.

14

THE CZECH SHOT

Hundreds of other equally complex stories exist, sometimes sad and sometimes happy, involving people who made it to the end of the war alive, one way or another. I am talking about my mother and, consequently, about myself, but I am going to revive another story, about a person I met later. I did not have much contact with him, although in a short time he became an unlikely hero in his role as villain. It so happened that somehow, Pavel, the Czech Jew (a false name because this story is not the same as the one told in public), became a friend of my parents and made his mark as a prisoner of war in the memories of all those who met him. I heard his terrifying personal account, and it made me realise that each person reacts in their own way, whatever that may be or whatever they may feel.

In the same way that Krisia and Andor were so unalike, she was withdrawn, whereas he was so chatty, yet had been made similar by the war, Pavel too told a forceful story.

Again, I know very little about his earlier past, before Theresienstadt, the concentration camp (sometimes called a ghetto) set up by the Nazis in Terezin, near Prague, the capital of Czechoslovakia at the time. For centuries, hundreds of thousands of Jewish people had lived in the provinces of Bohemia, Moravia and Silesia, subject to the varying moods of monarchs who reigned there. Some hated them, and others did not. The followers of the Pentateuch enjoyed moments of rare peace and prosperity in that particular region of Europe, interspersed, as always, with periods of violent persecution.

Like hatred, acceptance is a tree with shallow roots. It flourishes and flowers, but it is uprooted by the first strong wind. It is interesting that hatred exists in many societies with no solid or deep roots.

The difference is that hatred has enormous political power, much more than peaceful conviviality. People who come together in the name of a shared repulsion, even when they do not fully understand their own motives, tend to be easily manipulated. In the same way that mobs, hordes, throngs or rabbles enraptured by a band, a football team or any kind of passion are susceptible to varying degrees of contagion, they are drawn to the side that beckons them with the loudest, most seductive voice. And they are capable of anything.

Prague, a city with beautiful Baroque architecture, unique in the subtlety of its alleyways, squares and street corners, with 1,200 years of unbroken history and the windy Vltava (or the Moldau River) dividing it in two, had been the home of Jewish people for a long time. The Josefov neighbourhood, close to the city centre, was where they had lived for centuries. Sometimes, depending on the latest monarch, Josefov would be turned into a ghetto. At other times, it flourished as a fashionable neighbourhood. It is the home to many of the oldest synagogues in Europe and has a very small cemetery where so many generations have been buried that the tombstones have been crammed together chaotically. It is estimated that, in a small area, there are around 12,000 graves but that the number of Jewish people buried there since the 15th century is over 100,000. It is one of the oldest Jewish cemeteries in Europe.

Pavel was born in Bratislava, the current capital city of Slovakia, but he lived in Prague and was later taken to the camp in Theresienstadt. This was a kind of "model-camp", put together like an amusement park to entertain foreign visitors who had heard "stories" of supposed detention centres where Jewish people were treated like animals and killed like mosquitos.

It contained many areas dedicated to the most brazen propaganda. There were fake shops and cafés frequented by actors dressed as happy, pink-cheeked Jewish people. Officially the prisoners were allowed to go to the theatre and watch a children's opera called Brundibar, written by an inmate called Hans Krása.

The Red Cross accepted Hitler's invitation to visit the humanitarian detention centre, which was intended to serve as an example of what all the others were like.

Their representatives were allowed to visit prisoners in freshly painted quarters, where no more than three people slept in each bedroom.

This well-thought-out farce was the work of Hitler's Minister for Propaganda Joseph Goebbels, head marketer. It was so successful that the Nazis decided to make a documentary[1] in Theresienstadt in 1944. The objective seemed obvious – to present the travesty to the world. There was also the implicit advantage that, should the Allied forces win, the film could be a way of minimizing the force of the accusations that would certainly prevail.

A prisoner called Kurt Gerron directed it, under the close supervision of the Third Reich's propaganda bodies. And with plentiful resources, filming was over by the end of the year. In 1944, to complete the work with maximum efficiency, the director and all those who'd participated in filming were sent to Auschwitz and were murdered to avoid the farce being uncovered in the future.

The production had two names. One of them was *The Führer gives a city to the Jews,* which was so shameless it was substituted with *Theresienstadt: A documentary film from the Jewish settlement area.* Editing was never fully completed because of the speed at which the Allied Western forces advanced, but a number of scenes survived and were later used at international forums for the desired purpose.

A huge number of the 80,000 Czech Jews lost their lives at this exemplary prison.

Pavel was sent to the chimneys at Auschwitz but never got to enjoy its thermal comforts. The Germans were being intimidated by the proximity of the Red Army, so he and many others were gathered for one of the many "death marches" of the time, which were intended to drastically reduce the number of prisoners in extermination centres and perhaps employ them later in an effort to deter Hitler's enemies. Few of the debilitated prisoners managed to reach the destinations given by their captors. In the case of Pavel and his group, the end goal was the Mauthausen concentration camp, 20 kilometres from Linz, Austria. This, by the way, was the same place General Franco of Spain had sent a number of his enemies, captured during the Spanish Civil War, resulting in the deaths of 4,453 of them.

Pavel's detention at the new camp did not last long. Pavel recounts that the approach of the Americans was already palpable or, rather, that he could hear the movement of tanks, artillery fire and bombs exploding.

Following a decision by the camp commander, SS-Standartenführer Franz Ziereis, who was killed on 24 May by the troops who liberated the camp, German soldiers shot many prisoners because they dared to smile at the prospect of gaining their freedom.

Four or five days after fighting had been heard nearby, Mauthausen seemed to have been abandoned by fleeing guards. There were, however, a small number of Germans hidden in the area. Some impatient prisoners who could not wait to get out of those awful confines were killed as they tried to escape.

It was the end of May, the war in Europe was three days from conclusion, but fear persisted. Pavel and his friends remained in hiding for some time. They did not have the courage to move around and slept rough. He noted later, "It is interesting. [...] It was still cold, even in May, and there was snow on the ground. But it is even stranger that we managed to sleep soundly in those conditions because we felt like free men."

The prisoners slowly plucked up the courage to come out of hiding, as they could not see any opposition forces. The Czech citizen and his friends found a horse nearby. Starving, they killed it.

"That was my very first barbecue," he said years later, having settled in Brazil. The three friends, all of the same nationality, all bearers of extreme hatred of the Germans who had destroyed their families, prepared to walk to Prague, as Andor did to Budapest.

Freezing cold in that wintery May of 1945, the small shabby group lived through unconfessable experiences in the days to come (and so the need for a false name). Without any geographical or chronological precision, what we know is that on the journey, the former inmates came across a man lying in the snow, asleep under a dry tree.

They made their way towards him and saw that he was wearing the uniform of the Waffen-SS ("Schutzstaffel", literally Protection Squadron), Hitler's much-feared élite guard.

They shook him.

The man woke up and realised that before him stood prisoners on the loose, fugitives, and immediately said that he too was an escaped Jew and that he had stolen the uniform from a soldier to keep out the cold.

The ruse might have worked, but when they searched him, they found two rune lightning bolt insignia tattooed in his armpit. This was the mark of the SS which had, until recently, been a proud reminder of their absolute power. The parallel lightning bolts finally decided his lynching. He was stripped of his weapon and his uniform, which included hardwearing boots, a winter cape and all manner of military clothing. These were shared among the former inmates. The boys, aged between 14 and 15, used the semi-automatic Walther PPK, employed by the élite troop, to put an end to the German after they had kicked and beaten him. They felt no discomfort nor remorse.

Further on, I suppose once they were on Czech territory, the three former inmates were caught by Soviet soldiers who were on watch at a nearby prison. At this time, troops of varying nationalities occupied adjacent areas. Later they were divided up through political pacts. They were taken to the commander of the military prison and were identified as Jewish fugitives – their bony rib cages were undeniable proof – and they received a dignified welcome with food and intense chatter about the situation.

After the meal, the chief military officer took them to a metal mezzanine, surrounding a yard full of German soldiers, now prisoners themselves. As if by way of dessert, he proffered guns to the boys – maybe second-hand TT-33 pistols which the Soviets had many of at that time. Then he suggested they shoot a prisoner of their choice as revenge for the horror they had experienced. I do not know about the others, but Pavel acted promptly. Just as Amon Goeth had done, randomly in his dementia, Pavel fired a shot into the yard below.

A soldier, maybe a monster, maybe a common citizen who had been forced to participate in the conflict, fell bloody and lifeless. The commander took it a step further and encouraged the fugitive Jewish boy to go down and retrieve the bullet that had gone through the victim. Pavel took up the suggestion and did just that.

He is a peaceful man, from a nice, down-to-earth family. However, he still has the projectile used on that day. So we have to wonder whether these reactions provoke hostility among different peoples or whether it is the hostility between peoples that leads to this type of behaviour.

I do not dare to answer, and as far as I know, the man I met who was an intelligent person merely exercised what he considered to be his right to retaliate, in the same way that others chose silence, fear or the need to talk about the experiences they'd suffered. Again, what weighs against him –

and against everyone – is the fact that he belongs to a defective species, an error of breeding or evolution.

Long time later I met a young man who had named his son Pavel (or rather the real name) because he thought it right to honour the boy's courage and violent revenge. This is a rare gesture among the minorities captured during the European conflict.

15

THE FIFTH COLUMN

The Jewish people who were lucky enough to be in Brazil during the war had quite a different experience. My father was one of these people. He was the son of provident people who had left Berlin in 1932, immediately after Hitler's party entered the Reichstag (the German parliament) and shortly before his ascension to the command of the institution. To run away was dangerous too, but different and even fun. Before disembarking in Rio de Janeiro, my paternal grand-parents Ludwig and Rosalie and my father, a babe in arms, had tried to settle in France. They could not get work and, living off the soup handed out by volunteers to emigrants, soon sought a new destination.

I do not know about the refugee policy in Brazil at that time. I have no idea why they chose the country, but they told me that as they had no savings, they bought tickets to Rio on a cheap ship and, to make matters worse, in third class. My grandfather imagined the low standards that they would have to put up with during the crossing and used his last few pennies to buy a chamber pot.

This instrument was to be used by all three members of the family, principally by the child whose intestines were still weak and uncontrolled. As it turned out, this particular precautionary measure backfired. Once they were in their cramped cabin on board the ship, the name of which I never learned, the Heins discovered that the cubicle had four cramped bunks, with awful mattresses and no porthole through which to see the sea. There was, however, one creature comfort on board. Under each bunk the crew had taken the trouble to place two chamber pots. Therefore the one my grandfather had bought became a superfluous item and worse, a huge waste of money.

The pre-war period was a time of unclear ideologies, dangerous moods and vagueness for German refugees (and Jewish people). Brazil was the stage of huge political polarisation, with communists and fascists vying for central power. President Getúlio Vargas, who had led the 1930 revolution and assumed power of the country at that time, along with Juan Domingo Péron, in Argentina, was one of the *caudilhos* with an inclination for authoritarianism who thrived on the old continent. Both of them appeared to be seduced by the German dictator, and their flirtations were reciprocated. At the time the violent dictatorship of the new state had taken root (while my grandparents spoke stilted Portuguese), Vargas, who had become an unscrupulous despot and was armed with special powers, did not hesitate in sending the wife of his communist enemy Luís Carlos Prestes, Olga Benário, as a gift to the German Führer.

This decision must have made Hitler wild because the only thing worse than suffering from an abscessed anal fistula was to have to take in a Brazilian Jewish woman. To avoid upsetting anyone, Hitler asked his loyal Gestapo (*Geheime*

Staatspolizei, the Nazi political police), to take care of her. Olga was executed at the Berburg camp in 1942.

Until Brazil finally entered the war against the Germans in 1942, there was a certain convenient dubiety here, which earned Getúlio and the country, affection from the both the Allied powers and the Axis powers. Not that we had a powerful army. Brazil was of interest to both sides in the conflict due to its geopolitical position in that it had a long stretch of south Atlantic shoreline to offer its friends (whoever they were) and could provide a convenient base to access equatorial Africa.

For the German Jews, any turnaround in Brazilian foreign policy could have been dangerous. Germans who had immigrated to the south, and who had no Jewish ancestry, were strong supporters and even tried to influence Brazil's adherence to German ideals. In my grandfather's case, the first effect of Vargas's final decision to oppose the Nazis was cruel. He made a living as a travelling salesman. He was immediately identified as German because of both his accent and records on his original documents (without anyone caring that he was an escaped Jew) and lost his right to come and go. In other words, he would have to be a travelling salesman who did not travel, akin to being a tailor forbidden to use scissors and needles.

The upside of the story is that Brazil has always been the land of finding a way around problems. It was simply a question of tapping into that. As he did not have the necessary safe passage to allow him to take a train at Luz Station, the main railway station in São Paulo, Ludwig soon realised that if he got on the train at Lapa Station, a few stops earlier, he would not be checked. This was how his business prospered.

Many years later he told me that not everyone was so careless and that he was arrested by a policeman in Cuiabá after being reported, of course, by someone who'd noticed the "accent" of the "enemy". From jail he explained to his legal representative that he was Jewish and showed the word *Jüde* stamped on the photo-less identification document that he carried wherever he went around the country. The police officer was quick to retort, "And how do I know this document is yours?"

My grandfather immediately replied, "You can check," and proffered his thumb. His ID had been stamped with his fingerprints.

The suspicious official took my grandfather's thumb and compared it to the print on the piece of paper in an unprecedented exercise of dactyloscopy. He repeated his inspection three more times. Then he politely put the prisoner's arm back down, nodded and apologised. "You know how it is. If we are not careful, those Nazis will deceive the whole world."

My father and his brother, Franco, who was born in Rio de Janeiro, had settled in the São Paulo neighbourhood of Vila Mariana. In the coming years, they were enlisted in a group of scouts. Their mission was to walk the streets and ring the doorbells of those not complying with the blackout regulations in place at that time. During the war, although they were remote and unreachable targets for any kind of bombing raid, the largest state capitals in Brazil were kept in darkness to avoid an attack. It was not obligatory to turn off lights, but zealous citizens had to close windows and cover them with dark curtains. Inspection was carried out by the followers of Baden Powell, the founder of the scout movement (not the eminent bossa nova guitarist, who would only become famous many years later).

My father told me that he used to be careful when ringing the doorbells of disobedient residents. When the door opened and he was asked why he was there, he would answer hesitantly that they had to close their curtains. Some disobeyed; others did not.

"Go to hell, brat!" was the most polite response he received during his times as a blackout inspector.

As for my *carioca* uncle, he had no idea at that time what it meant to be Jewish or German, and neither was he bothered about the matter. So when he was annoyed, he quickly learned to say to my father, who was born in Berlin, "You fifth column rascal." Fifth column was an expression used to refer to groups and individuals who worked in a country or region, helping the enemy by spying and spreading subversive propaganda.

Besides the families and friends of the 450 conscripts, 13 officers and eight pilots in the Brazilian Expeditionary Force (FEB) who had lost their lives in the real war, the conflict in Brazil consisted of a series of irrelevant, even funny, episodes such as the one described above.

War is war, they say. They mean it is nothing, and life goes on.

I shall make a digression here to talk about the role of my grandmother Rosalie in this passage of history. We always called her Rosel. She was a trained nurse and was very proud of the diploma she was awarded at a Berlin university. Sometime after she had arrived in Rio de Janeiro, she was hired to take care of a Jewish children's home in the neighbourhood of Cosme Velho. This institution still exists but was set up specifically to take in orphaned or abandoned children who had come to Brazil when the Nazi movement no longer offered any guarantee for the lives of those it despised.

So while my grandfather travelled from Manaus to Leticia, in Colombia along the Amazon River, selling whatever trinkets he had managed to pick up in the port in Rio, Rosel was the guardian angel of numerous lost children, becoming a substitute mother to a number of them. A boy called Manfred Korytowsky was among them. Years after he was cradled and cared for by the nurse from Berlin, he returned to Europe. First he went to the Middle East, became a paratrooper for the State of Israel and fought in Israel's army in many wars in the region. Later, while living in post-Nazi Germany, he became a filmmaker and was known as the German Walt Disney because of a character he created called Pumückl (a children's hero in Germany). He continued to worship my grandmother Rosel, as though she were his real mother, until he died in 1999.

Manfred, or Mani as we called him, had numerous machine gun bullets in his body, the result of the role he had played on 8 May 1972 when he was one of the passengers onboard Sabena flight 571 (a Belgian airline) that was hijacked by terrorists of the Palestinian organisation Black September. On the apron of Lod Airport (now called Ben Gurion), extremists threatened to blow up the aircraft and passengers if the Israeli government did not free 315 of its "comrades in the struggle" who were being held in the country.

Mani saw an assault group disguised as mechanics moving closer to the jet with the aim of quashing the kidnappers. Two future prime ministers of Israel were in the rescue party – Ehud Bark and Benjamin Netanyahu, who was hit in the shoulder.

When the soldiers entered the aeroplane, shouting at everyone to get down, one of the terrorists, standing next to the future film-maker, grabbed a grenade and was just about to detonate it. Mani, reports said, jumped on top of the man, and they were both hit by a number of shots fired from machine gun.

The action led to the deaths of the kidnappers and left the boy, who had been cared for by my grandmother, on the brink of death. He became a national hero and was visited by the prime minister at the time, Golda Meir. He received the commendations he deserved for his heroism.

He never tired of saying that, having survived the hardship of a war and a terrorist attack, he was convinced that the Jewish people would never have the peace they yearned for, even in the land that had been given to them by the United Nations (given back to them, some would say).

16

A COAT OF PAINT FOR POPEYE

In 1960, Ludwig Hein's house in the region of the Guarapi-ranga reservoir had a peculiarity that was of dubious taste. In the middle of the front garden, between the veranda and the boundary wall, was a life-size statue of the character Popeye, created by Elzie Crisler Segar. Nobody knows who put the spinach eater there, but it was certainly not Ludwig, as he bought the house after it was built, with all its features, most of which were very tasteful.

There is a photo of this period in which my mother can be seen painting the cartoon character, which had become rather shabby and was peeling. It is a curious picture because Krisia looks happy with her task, although she was never one for manual work and never learned to cook, embroider or knit, activities that are usually picked up in childhood. As we know, she was imprisoned throughout her childhood.

In the photo she looks unusually serene as she gives Popeye a fresh coat of paint. She was about 28 or 29 years old and already spoke good Portuguese, although I may be mistaken, as I was much older when I realised that my mother had always had a strong Polish accent. It sounded like flawless Portuguese to her young son.

That was Ludwig's third house in the reservoir region and his first on the peninsula, which is still called the Riviera Paulista. The Germans and Italians who summered there called it Santo Amaro. Most of them chose the reservoir near São Paulo to practice water sports, rest and socialise with their neighbours without having to travel too far. The reservoir is less than 30 kilometres from the centre of the São Paulo capital. It was a short trip, the only inconvenience being the deserted, muddy road. At that time, the water in the Guarapiranga (in Tupi-Guarani, *guara* means heron and *piranga* red) was clean and transparent, perfect for swimming, water skiing and sailing.

I remember that Sven, who was still strong, although he already complained of the pain I shall talk about later, used to swim from my grandfather's house to the dam, which was two or three kilometres away, and back. In fact, and this is still true, the owners of land on the waterfront had the right to use the area between their land and the water and were responsible for its upkeep, although officially these areas belong either to the water board or the electricity board, both being beneficiaries of the great reservoir.

On the shoreline, in front of the house watched over by Popeye, were some small wooden boats used for rowing trips. Nearby, however, there were all sorts of vessels, some with cabins, some without, some big and some small, almost all of them covered with a thick tarpaulin used at that time and tied to fixed buoys anchored to the muddy reservoir floor.

From the terrace of Ludwig's house, two objects in the shape of aeroplanes could also be seen resting in the inlet. They too were covered with tarpaulin to protect them from the elements. The aeroplanes were Republic RC-7 *Seabees*, small amphibious aircraft used by one of my grandfather's neighbours for panoramic flights over the water, mostly taking tourists from the city.

The owner of the planes, Herbert, was a skilful aviator and apparently an excellent mechanic. When he was not airborne, either because he had no passengers or because of adverse meteorological conditions, he could be seen strolling around the Riviera, often in the company of his very blond children, their Caucasian features matching everyone else's in the neighbourhood. Over time, and my memory is of far-off days and is irrelevant, as I was only five years old at the time, Herbert and Ludwig grew closer. This was the objective of those who lived or spent the weekends in the bucolic region of the reservoir.

My grandfather was fond of Scottish whisky. He drank Old Parr and smoked cigars. Herbert soon found this out, as he also enjoyed the Caledonian liquor. They were around the same age and both communicated better in German than in Portuguese.

On that veranda overlooking the Popeye given a coat of paint by Krisia and the large main lake of the reservoir, beyond which some buildings could be seen in the distant city, Ludwig and Herbert weaved long conversations. I recall that with a pair of binoculars, it was even possible to tell the time on the then Willys clock on the roof of the Conjunto Nacional. Later it became the Ford clock and even later the Itaú clock.

I do not believe the two neighbours became any more than drinking buddies, but they often met when my grandfather was in Santo Amaro.

I know very little of their discussions, but politics, the economy and the war (which had ended only 15 years earlier) were subjects that must have been on the menu, accompanied by whisky and appetizers. I heard, and this was a decade later, that Herbert had stated he was Jewish and that he had left Europe before the situation got worse; as such, he too had walked the path that Ludwig had.

As the Brazilian saying goes, "One goose recognises another goose." (Maybe it is a different bird?) As their discussions went on, my grandfather began to question his conversation partners Semitic roots. He could not tell me why he started to doubt Herbert's sincerity. The odd comment, slightly unfamiliar expressions and other indications that the aviator was not who he said he was started to emerge.

Jewish survivors or even emigrants, as was Ludwig's case, were always on the back foot regarding other foreigners at that time. This was around the same period that the Mossad – the Israeli intelligence service – captured Adolf Eichmann. He lived in San Fernando, Argentina, and worked in a German manufacturing company. He had changed his name but lived in constant fear of being discovered as being one of the masterminds among the war criminals. He was the engineer responsible for the logistics of the extermination carried out by Nazi Germany.

In 1960, under the codename Ricardo Klement, Eichmann was kidnapped by Mossad agents, secretly held in prison in Buenos Aires until he could be illegally transported to Israel, where he was put on trial in 1961 and hanged the following year.

Cases like Eichmann's were seen in South America for some decades and included both major and minor war criminals, ranging from concentration camp guards up to their commanders. One of the most wanted Nazis, the doctor, Joseph Mengele, responsible for evil experiments on humans imprisoned in Auschwitz, also found his way to the continent. He lived in Argentina, later Brazil, and managed to avoid being recognised by employing a variety of artifices. Indeed, it is said that the so-called angel of death spent some time in the environs of the Riviera, but history reveals he actually lived in the region of the other reservoir, Billings, in a neighbourhood called Eldorado, now part of the municipality of Diadema.

The fact is that he died on a beach in Bertioga in 1979 after suffering a stroke while swimming. It is believed that his death was agony, far less painful, however, than those he inflicted on child prisoners in Auschwitz under the pretext of carrying out genetic research. Mengele was buried in Embu das Artes, a municipality of Greater São Paulo, under the name Wolfgang Gerhard, one of the many he used during his lifetime. This was a combination of two common German first names, precluding any chance of identification. Later, in 1985, following investigations, his body was exhumed and his death was finally confirmed. The final resting place of the doctor of human guinea pigs was revealed by the Stammer family whom he lived with for some time and with whom he even bought a country home in the town of Caieiras.

It was therefore around the time of Eichmann's imprisonment and trial that the whisky-soaked conversations between Ludwig and Herbert must have provoked the latter's first pro-Nazi comments, somewhat unexpected coming from a self-declared Jew.

One particular night, Ludwig astutely bought extra bottles of Old Parr and steered Herbert to destabilisation, in other words, to getting drunk, muddling his words, loosening his tongue and becoming aggressive. Ludwig led the conversation to the subject that had alerted him, slowly diluting his own drink in sparkling water; he finally heard Herbert affirm that the Jews were "sons of bitches" and that he regretted not having done away with them all when he lived in Latvia, his homeland. The full name of the careless drinker was Herbert Cukurs.

He was a competent aviator, and before the war he was even thought of as a kind of Latvian Charles Lindbergh. He flew inconceivably long distances in a wooden C6 monoplane equipped with a Havilland Gipsy engine. He flew from Latvia to Gambia and on another occasion to Tokyo. In 1933, he was awarded the Harmon trophy by his compatriots, which was only given to extremely successful adventure heroes.

He could have gone down well in history, as attested to by his initial conversations with my grandfather, but only up to a certain quantity of whisky. There are hundreds of witness accounts of the hero's enthusiasm for the task of eliminating the Jewish people from his country. German authorities chose him as a trustworthy national leader. He ultimately was responsible for the deaths of thousands of innocent civilians, under the command of the SD, a Nazi security and intelligence unit. Cukurs drowned 1,200 Latvians Jews in a lake close to the capital of his country. He also led the assassination of 10,600 people in a forest on the outskirts of Riga, massacred thousands more in Rumbula and burned down synagogues, always ensuring that the Jewish people of the respective community were locked inside. As he never stood trial, there was some doubt about his behaviour during the war when he earned the awful (but maybe fair) nickname of the Butcher of Riga.

In 1965, Herbert, who was a big strong man, was lured to Uruguay. Although the invitation seemed somewhat suspicious, he accepted it from a businessman who wanted to offer tourist flights between Montevideo and Buenos Aires. Cukurs — the prospective partner assured — was to play a fundamental role in setting up a business that would make him rich.

The invitation was a trap set by the Mossad, and when he arrived in the pleasant capital city of the former Cisplatine Province, Cukurs was put in a car boot and taken to a house deemed to be safe. This was the same procedure that the Israeli secret service had adopted during the capture of Eichmann. It is said that the captors' objective was again to take the presumed criminal to Israel for trial. But Cukurs, with the muscles of a Latvian butcher/aviator, fought back and knocked some of them down before being shot dead on 23 February 1965.

Up until today, Latvia and Cukurs' Brazilian relatives dispute or simply deny the guilt of the man who drank Old Parr on my grandfather's terrace. The fact that he was never officially tried gives him the right to be presumed innocent, despite the many witnesses who talk about his actions in Latvia during the war. There are also those who say Ludwig told the story of a certain drinking binge to the people of the São Paulo Jewish community who had links to the Israeli intelligence service.

The statue painted by Krisia, which still exists and is probably in need of another coat of paint, saw the whole thing.

17

A DISTANT RETREAT

Jewish boys usually have a Bar Mitzvah, a religious coming of age, at 13 years of age. This is almost always a family celebration, with lots of presents – mostly books – and music, and the ceremony commemorates the fact that Judaism is being passed on to the next generation.

Many of the ceremonies the more religious groups hold have long extracts from the Pentateuch – the five books of the Torah – the meaning of which is often indecipherable, principally among the less religious Jews, who do not speak Hebrew and are not familiar with the narrative of the so-called sacred writings.

For this group, the Bar Mitzvah is just a secular rite of passage that has little to do with God or with religion. They sing their *Parashah* (the extract, or portion, in numerical order that they have been assigned for their coming of age), often unaware of the meaning that religious people attribute to that passage from the Torah and really just want to get to the opening of the presents. It could be about the roof of some biblical temple, an unknown passage of the Jewish epic in the desert or about the time there was no yeast, and unleavened bread was invented. This is the matzah eaten on the festive days of the community.

Jewish people who are born here but do not attend schools specifically for the community do not have the chance or desire to learn the language of their ancestors, so to them, the rabbi's words in Hebrew just sound like harsh noises, and unlike foreign films, there are no subtitles. The same went for Catholics who did not speak Latin when it was the language of the Mass, not so long ago.

When they have their Bar Mitzvahs, Jewish men gain the right to wear the *tallit,* a silk shawl that separates the men from the boys, in religious terms. As they are officially adults after the ceremony, they have the right to participate in special occasions like weddings, funerals, worship and communitarian circumcisions, which require the presence of ten Jewish adult men (nowadays I hear that liberal communities accept women to make up the quorum).

In November 2019, months after his 91st birthday, Andor Stern, my father-in-law, was invited by Rabbi David Weitman of São Paulo's oldest synagogue – the Kehilat Israel in the Bom Retiro neighbourhood – to become an unprecedented late Bar Mitzvah. This was more a recognition on the part of the community than a rite of passage. The Memorial for Jewish Immigration and the Holocaust is located in the same building as the synagogue. As it had been impossible for Andor to become an adult Jew during the Second World War, he was given this special right. He was spared the need to memorise a Parashah. In a ceremony attended by family members, the Brazilian press and even the BBC, he became the world's oldest person to have a Bar Mitzvah.

His celebration was unlike the standard ones around the world. The rabbi called Andor to the pulpit. Andor then repeated some blessings that the religious leader gave him and donned the phylacteries (*tefillin* in Hebrew), two strips of leather to which two small boxes are attached, containing scrolls of parchment inscribed with specific extracts from the Torah, to protect the wearer and create a symbolic connection between him and God.

One of the boxes is tied to the participant's forehead. The strips of the other box are tied to his right arm, and the box is placed in his right hand. And that was it; once the accessories had been put in place, Andor Stern's Bar Mitzvah was over. The rabbi, the singer and other people standing nearby took him by the hand and started to dance to two traditional songs from the recently assembled Hebrew songbook. The accidental Brazilian, raised in Hungary, smiled and tried to sing along to the words (which he did not know), and from one second to the next, he belonged to the religion and the ethnicity that were the reason his life had hung by a thread during the war in Europe.

Many photographers registered the unique ceremony, and lenses flickered from all sides.

The photo chosen by the rabbi to display on the screen up on the stage contained some shocking features. It showed Andor's arm tattooed with the number from Auschwitz framed by the strips of the phylacteries. Rabbi Weitman, in tears, told the assembled believers that that was the first time in his life he had placed the sacred strips on an arm that had been permanently tarnished with the Nazi inscription. Symbolically, he added, the strips over the tattoo proved that God had prevailed over the antisemites.

The 91-year-old Jewish man also cried.

The event at Kehilat Israel was the unexpected end to a story of fear and denial spanning five decades. Neither the rabbi, nor those in attendance, had any idea of the importance of the moment they had just witnessed.

Although Andor Stern's name is common among Ashkenazic Jews, he came to Brazil set on never again mentioning his origins to anyone at all. Because of them, he had suffered since he was a child, witnessing a cruel war and experiencing the bitter taste of seeing his relatives (including his mother) exterminated by the Nazis.

In his former life, Jewish had just been an adjective (and not a noun) that meant bad, unacceptable, to be suppressed. So why insist on preserving this flaw? Since his childhood in Hungary, Andor and other Jewish people had been segregated and mistreated by classmates and teachers for their ethnic/religious condition.

To guarantee distance from Israelis living in São Paulo, Andor used a protective shield and some personal guidelines. The shield was his Brazilian passport. The personal guidelines were to start a new life far from any vestiges of the religion to which he had previously belonged. He made friends with Brazilians, Hungarians and Germans, and when there was a Jewish person around, he steered clear.

For more than a decade, he ignored Bom Retiro, the neighbourhood where most of the São Paulo Jewish community lived (nowadays the Jewish residents have largely been substituted by Korean immigrants) and the place where his late Bar Mitzvah would take place 60 years later.

Denying his origin and keeping a distance from his fellow men were weapons he used so his new life would not carry the scars of the first one. It worked. After learning to work with card perforators at IBM, (International Business Machines) which was later revealed to have been a big collaborator in the systematisation of the extermination of European Jews – he went to work at São Paulo Tramway, Light and Power Company, or simply Light, as it was known to the electricity consumers of São Paulo and in most of Brazil, and met the woman he was to marry. She was called Therezinha (in the diminutive, like Krisia) and was an employee at the Canadian company. She was a true Brazilian and had no connection whatsoever with Judaism or any remotely "perilous" ancestry. These are important facts in understanding that period.

They first met in 1952, and the wedding took place in 1954 at the Santo Antonio do Pari church in the Roman Catholic tradition.

For the young Jewish escapee, to marry in a religious institution of a different faith was further evidence that his former life had disappeared in the mists of time. When Andor and Therezinha were setting up home together, in a house in front of the São Paulo Prison, in the neighbourhood of Carandiru, they sought the services of a Jewish man whom Andor deemed harmless.

His name was Jaime. He was a travelling furniture salesman from whom the groom bought a bed, a mattress and a wardrobe. Jaime was one of the many so-called Service Jews, a generic designation for door-to-door salesmen who were sometimes Syrian or Lebanese or from other parts of the Middle East –"Turks", as they were known.

Therezinha was settling up with Jaime when he told her he was sure her future husband was Jewish and that she would "soon" have proof. The unwarranted comment seemed obvious to the salesman, as Andor, like it or not, had always had stereotypically Jewish features. And as I said before, "One goose recognises another goose."

The information was of no importance at all to the future wife of the survivor in denial. All the São Paulo middle class knew was that Jewish people ate with their hats on. That was what they said, although it was rather unfounded and seemed more like a legend. Andor did not eat with his hat on (few of his countrymen did); therefore, he could not be a Jew, although she was not concerned one way or the other.

It was only later that Therezinha understood that the "soon" contained in Jaime's announcement was a reference to the circumcision Andor must have undergone as a Jewish boy. That was the discovery she was certain to make. The information was quite without meaning for the virgin bride-to-be, who had never seen any type of male sex organ, from any origin, and as such would not have been in a position to make a comparison.

The life of the couple followed its natural course. At the time they married, they already had three children in their care: Therezinha's younger sister whom she had adopted and two orphaned nephews who were also in her charge. Andor, who worked a great deal, never talked about his past, and Therezinha continued to work when she could, as they later had two children themselves, making a total of five children bringing joy (or not, with all the mess) to the Stern household.

The episode of Adolf Eichmann's arrest brought up memories of the former Jew's past. He had never told his wife, as a confession or as news, that he belonged to the "chosen people", but his behaviour started to change with the capture of the Nazi leader who had been presumed dead. A short time after this event, Andor started to speculate over the destiny of his father, formerly István, who had divorced his mother and disappeared into the frontiers of the European conflict.

When Andor found him – again the Red Cross enters this story, assisting in the search – his father had changed his name. He was living in Burgos, Spain, and like his son, he was trying to live a new life. The discovery came as quite a shock to Andor's Spanish half-brothers who had many questions about their father's past. As he never talked about his past, Esteban, as he was then called, could have lived in the shadows or, worst-case scenario, he could be a rehabilitated criminal. His children were already nurturing these suspicions when they met Andor, who was introduced as "Esteban's nephew". However, the extraordinary similarity between the Spanish son Carlos and Andor did not go unnoticed.

Under pressure, the visitor, Andor, ended up confessing that he was a Hungarian Jew and the son of the man he was visiting.

"*No, judio, no!*" The brothers were shocked and disbelieving at the news that, therefore, they too had Jewish blood.

It is important to note that in Spain, several centuries ago, Jewish people, Muslims and Christians all lived together for around 700 years, without any hostilities. In fact, this harmony led to enormous human, artistic, philosophical and architectural progress. Following the expulsion of the Moors and the Jewish people, carried out at the end of the 15th century by the Catholic kings (1492), everyone was forced to flee. Those who stayed faced the rigours of the Inquisition, which led to the deaths of thousands of undesirables. After this period, the number of Jewish people living in Spain could be counted on the fingers of one hand. The situation was not much better at the time when Andor visited his father, Spain being under the command of the ever-so-Catholic General Franco. Indeed, things have not really changed much, even today.

At that juncture, it became impossible for Andor to continue denying his origins. And nothing changed when his wife found out; after all, he continued to participate in family meals without his hat.

In the future, the Jewish man born in Brazil who had escaped from Auschwitz was to say it was impossible for anyone to run away from what they have once been. By an inexplicable coincidence in a world with so few remaining Jewish people and, above all, in a country where they have always represented less than 1 per cent of the population (there are a little over 100,000 Jewish people living in Brazil), both Andor's daughters married members of the community he would have loved to have forgotten. The coincidence is even greater because neither of the girls frequented any Jewish club, school or environment. So it was divine provocation from which Andor Stern was not lucky enough to escape.

This is why the late Bar Mitzvah of Brazilian Jewish history, which took place in the neighbourhood he had tried hard to avoid for so many years, was even more emotional than the people in attendance at São Paulo's oldest Israeli synagogue that day could ever have imagined.

18

THE POPE'S LAWYER

By the mid-1960s, Oskar Schindler was no longer a successful industrialist. In fact, he had driven his last businesses into liquidation, including his final bold venture, a cement factory. To make matters worse, he had a heart attack in 1964. Although he was still relatively young at 55, he never completely recovered financially. He mainly lived off the donations made by Jewish people he had saved, known as the *Schindlerjüden* (literally, Schindler Jews).

This was the year that Krisia received the news that her father, Teodor, had not died. Actually, there is conflicting information on this. Some say that father and daughter had known about each other since the end of the war, and that, nevertheless, Teodor had preferred his daughter stay with her Brazilian uncle and aunt, as he felt unable to provide peace and comfort in chaotic post-war Krakow, which was already under Soviet rule, and people's movements were restricted. This hypothesis emerged much later and was repeated in Krisia's account at the Shoah Foundation. As it never came up in my childhood, I prefer to leave it to one side.

Children, as I was at the time, always know who and where their grandparents are. Neither my sister nor I ever heard a single word about the existence of this Polish grandfather when we were little. Neither did we see the correspondence from Poland that my mother later spoke about in the recording she did for the Shoah Foundation.

As I cannot think of any reason she would omit this information, I prefer to stick to the earlier story, remembered and believed by the rest of the family, that Krisia, unaccustomed to the cameras, had suffered a memory lapse during her account to the Shoah foundation.

In the original story, which I have no qualms about holding onto in my memory, I have a vague idea that someone (I do not know who) who lived in Brazil, went to Krakow for some unknown reason and bumped into my grandfather in the centre of the city, in a pedestrian precinct.

This may appear to be an unlikely coincidence, but everyone who was around then is now dead, so I will never know the true story. I confess there are a number of reasons that make that meeting implausible. The principal one is that at the height of the Cold War, the so-called Iron Curtain was almost impenetrable. A huge amount of bureaucracy was required to visit a country in the Soviet region, and anyone who visited became a suspect in the eyes of the Brazilian military dictatorship, which did not like to see its inhabitants on Communist territory.

Krakow is not a small city either. It has almost one million inhabitants (including the surrounding municipalities), and to run into someone who has been presumed dead for decades (and recognise them) is the storyline for a melodrama – the nature of which is to use exaggeration as a means of evoking emotional reactions.

The fact is that somehow my mother found out that her father, who was believed to have disappeared in 1939, was alive and in the city where they were both born. He was using the name Tadeusz Polanowski, a very common name in the land of Chopin and ideal for hiding his Jewish ancestry. (It is worth noting in the light of the last two chapters that people's original names are often the defenceless victims of wartime.)

This should have been an important event in my boyhood, but it was not, although I can recall it happening. In fact, at that time, all my attention was focused on my father who had undergone surgery (with the medical resources available at that time), after suffering from stabbing pains in his back for years. He was subjected to sessions of cobalt therapy (the medical use of high-energy gamma rays, from a source of radioactive cobalt 60, to destroy cancer cells). After the operation, he was thin, his body was not reacting to treatment and he became disillusioned. He had suffered with pain since his youth and had put up with all the different kinds of rudimentary treatment that existed then. The worst of these, which he often talked about, was called "traction", a kind of artificial stretching involving the use of weights and pulleys that were supposed to decompress the vertebra and provide relief.

This treatment is used in physiotherapy and is somewhat reminiscent of the "pau-de-arara" (literally parrot's perch), a method of torture used to extract confessions from prisoners. It was often used on political prisoners during the military dictatorship (the one that lasted from 1964 to 1984). It is said that it is effective in uncomplicated cases. But it was not in my father's case. He spent several months in traction in Germany, accompanied by my grandmother Rosel – who you will remember was a student nurse and believed in the healing skills of German medicine – forgetting the still recent behaviour of the nation.

Unfortunately, the result was disappointing, and all subsequent attempts were also in vain until the aggressive surgery that almost killed him in his 60s. It is said that at that time, not even my grandparents nurtured any hope that he would survive.

With Krisia's determined support and her refusal to accept bad prognoses, Sven convalesced. During his many months of recovery, considered unlikely by the doctors, he was kept in a São Paulo hospital.

Because of this, my sister and I moved to Ludwig and Rosel's house for those long months. Information about the disease was sparse, visits were not allowed and nobody talked about the matter in the house. This was meant to protect us from the harsh reality, but naturally this attitude just caused us distress and fear.

Thus the information about the existence of a grandfather I had never seen was irrelevant and went unnoticed by us and by my mother, who was focussed at all on times on her sick husband's convalescence.

I later wrote about my father and his illness in a text for a book called *Aprendi com meu pai (I Learned with My Father),* in which a number of people wrote about the relationships they had with their fathers. Before resuming the story of Krisia and Teodor's reunion, I would like to reproduce that piece of writing here:

My father was Sven. He was named after a Scandinavian poet and adventurer and this made him unique. No-one else in Brazil had a father with the same name as mine. I do not know what affect names have on people, but he too became a poet.

He did not write poetry, but he brought charm and emotion into our lives. His eyes sang, his gestures were rich rhymes, his dignity was unwavering and he moved like Alexandrine verse.

I have another image of him, maybe it is more fitting. Sven was not a poet, he was poetry.

Created out of pain, like the best poetry.

He was already ill before I was born. He suffered from what people generically term, backache.

They stretched and pulled him, opened him up from the nape of his neck down to the dip of his buttocks. The pain never ceased.

But he was strong and handsome and he worked. He was always smiling. I remember – I must have been very young – a scene in an old amusement park on Avenida Santo Amaro. Sven took me to the carousel in the Parque Imperial there. It was near my house, for years. I rode round, proud to see him as I went past each time, his encouraging blue eyes made me feel like a general on an illustrious Rocinante.

One time I came back around and his smile had given way to a mask of pain. The pain, always the pain. I think that was the first time I noticed it. I was afraid of falling off on the next turn that seemed to last forever. But when I came back around, on my metallic steed, he was smiling again. He was like that throughout his whole life.

One day, they took me away from my father. They took away his songs, the harmonica he played, his jokes and magic tricks. My sister and I were exiled at my grandmother's house while he went to "take care of his back".

"Children have to eat everything, not know everything," was my dear grandmother's favourite phrase that was always delivered in a strong German accent. So, we did not eat – we did not know.

Now I know that my father was in hospital for six months. They discovered he had a tumour in the medulla. They bombarded him with cobalt and he became disillusioned.

And we ate.

It was the 1960s. He was in his early thirties. Surgical and post-surgical techniques were in their infancy.

My father was dying and we ate.

One morning, they took us home.

An ambulance stopped at the door and I watched as they put a thin frail man on a sort of sedan-chair. Strong nurses carried him down the steps to his bedroom. I shouted out to him. He drew himself up and was taken inside saying: "The Emperor has arrived."

Months of silences followed, cups of tea, visits and soups. My father came back to life.

He was happy again and made us happy. He was transparent like the best poems. You could tell when he was delighted and when he was upset. He cried with joy when we were all together at our country home, singing in the moonlight. He bestowed kisses and affection on my mother. But the pain persisted.

It never left him.

The operation severed many nerve endings. We all knew that one day his legs would stop working.

There would be walking sticks. Later, a wheelchair. He kept his humour and strength to work.

I always sensed, however, that poems forged from pain end sadly. And so, Sven became bitter. The walking sticks came. The wheel-

chair. Exile to Campos do Jordão, because big cities are cruel to those who cannot walk.

He was still in pain, and no matter how much I waved from the carrousel, I could no longer make him smile.

His dignity remained unwavering like an Alexandrine verse. But the poetry was ending. I learned with my father that the best poems are born out of pain.

And that they die.

The father/daughter reunion only received serious consideration once Sven had recuperated. I think it was in 1966 or 1967, although the exact date is of no importance to the story. Some intense preparations were required, and letters were exchanged – I remember this because I collected stamps – plane tickets were purchased and my mother in particular braced herself.

Meeting a father who had been presumed dead, 30 years after what had seemed like a permanent separation, could potentially be a disaster. What was he like, the man who had become a major and jumped on his horse to win a war that was lost in two days? How had his emotions changed? How had his life turned out after he was widowed and lost his only daughter?

Some doubts were dissipated by letter. The story of his change of name, for example. His daughter was told that he had married under the new name, after the war, to a woman who already had a small child. He also said that he was still working as a lawyer in his firm in Krakow and, of course, they discussed all the details of my mother's trip. For his part, Teodor received the news that my mother was married with two children and led a very different life in Brazil than the one of her childhood in Poland.

Names, times and places had changed. It remained to be seen – and this would only happen face to face – whether attitudes, behaviour and feelings were still the same. Could three decades of war, political turbulence and gaps in knowledge have the effect of transforming people, even those who had precious family ties?

In Brazil, it was decided that Krisia would travel with her husband, not only because he was as excited as she was by that time, but also for practical reasons. To lift a corner of the Iron Curtain and cross it may not prove to be a straightforward touristic experience in those days. The journey was a kind of crossing into the unknown, with the potential to expose the traveller to unknown safety issues and even behaviour in a divided world, subject to all sorts of idiosyncrasies.

In 2004, an opportunity arose for me to visit the city founded in 1257 and ruled by Prince Krak (hence the name Krakow, Cracóvia in Portuguese). Long before Nazi domination, it had suffered a number of other invasions. The first of these was legendary and involved the existence of a monster in the area, which caused death and destruction at the end of the Middle Ages. It came to be known as the Wawel Dragon because it was said to have gone on the rampage at the site of a hill of the same name on the banks of the Vistula. A castle, the symbol of Poland, was built there, and it is one of the most valuable architectural complexes in the nation.

A short time after spending a week investigating Krakow, I produced a piece of writing called *Café Hawelka*, seen below, in which I talk about the sensations I had, some of which I have expressed in previous chapters.

I do not know how it ended. It must have been rushed, with no time for hugs or farewells, perhaps not even a look. I imagine it is like that in wartime. The sound of booms, shouts and orders are heard. An officer is anxious to leave, to fight for his country, a country without woods, or sea, just two frightened pairs of eyes in a room in Warsaw.

"Warsaw," she told me, this was in fact one of the few things she told me because she did not like to remember, "Warsaw is safer," the major assured them, in his capacity as father, not as a military man. Father.

Neither do I know how he left, except for the unquestionable fact that he was riding a handsome horse. The mother and daughter stayed behind, crushed by the persistent silence of the bombings, gunshots and agonized voices.

Everyone knows fathers are never wrong. But the same cannot be said of Majors. They swept through Warsaw. Krakow, where they lived, suffered badly, but far less. They had to hide almost immediately. The Major, the poor Major.

One day I found out that he was not really a major. He was a lawyer; he had a legal firm and clients. During the war, however, manual labourers become soldiers, clerks become lieutenants and lawyers become Majors. Poor Major of the court of justice. He mounted his horse (I wonder if he knew how to ride), sat up straight and went into battle against the panzers. Or maybe it was quite different from this?

My story is theirs. They who were removed. Transported, Confined. Concentrated. My mother's mother, Felicja – how old was she? 30? 32? And her daughter who was just eight years old and had not yet learned the declensions of written Polish and would not need them for years. All she needed were her hands to cling to the skirts, then rags and later uniforms of her mother, who never left her.

Everyone knows what happened. She was Spielberg's red dot on the widescreen of my life much later on. I am referring to the daughter because I never saw the mother, only in photos from before the war – photos are the least of what is lost when it is all over.

One day I went to Washington where there is one of these museums about those truly incredible years. Before leaving I asked about Bergen-Belsen. The last camp, after Auschwitz, that they survived. After Plaszów, which they sailed through. It was a walk in the park after the ghetto.

The woman responsible for the Documentation Centre was helpful, but seemed unhappy with what she found. A single photo. "There was a typhoid epidemic when the British arrived." She regretted. "People were dying, a lot of people were dying. They had to burn everything." She regretted even more – and I could almost see my grandmother's face in that mass of people. The woman who resisted until the last day of the war, who must have remembered the lawyer turned Major in her agony, and who I always imagine dying while smiling for her daughter, who was free.

She gave me the photo. A photocopy of the photo. A group of children squeezed together in a large warehouse. Squeezed together through habit. It struck me that the focus was perfect. "It was a professional." I deduced, thinking vaguely of Churchill, with his gin and cigars, the Commander in Chief of the British battalions responsible for liberating the camp.

The fourth girl from the right in the second row. The fourth girl from the right in the second row. The fourth girl from the right in the second row. The fourth girl from the right in the second row.

"My mother." I stammered and, stunned, walked out into the frozen twilight of the American Federal District.

It was the Red Cross that removed her from that scene and from that setting. Squalid, suffering from tuberculosis and an orphan. I have no idea how these things work, but the fact is that she ended up in Malmö, in Sweden. A sanitorium. A place for sick children with no records.

When wars end, the winners create methods of normalisation. These are usually long, bureaucratic and slow. One day, we all know, the pieces fall back into place. At least some of them. Others will be forgotten and washed away by the weather. And the weather, like the rain that causes mudslides, will change the landscape.

The Red Cross decided to publish lists of survivors. It relied on the benevolence of the big international newspapers, and slowly information appeared on who was where. I have no idea whether it was a Sunday edition; I do not know which month or year. One day, however, her name appeared in the New York Times. Tovek came across it. When I was little I heard people calling him JT. He was my Bergen-Belsen grandmother's brother.

JT found my mother.

The reader of the New York Times was struggling. I do not know what he did; I know everyone did something in those days. He had a sister living in São Paulo though. She and her husband had wisely fled before the war and were thriving in the land of Getúlio. She was my grandmother (the only maternal grandmother I knew and who I loved dearly) Antonina, Nusia, I miss her.

There are a number of sub-dramas in this story that I will never know. The important point is that the little girl from the Malmö *sanitorium was soon put on a transatlantic ship headed for the Santos coastline.*

These were the golden years. Learning. Integration. Glenn Miller. Rejection and love. A new beginning in a still vibrant São Paulo.

Her wedding on the mezzanine of Sears (the shop's slogan - "satisfaction guaranteed or your money back"). Me. My sister.

I have the elegant black and white wedding photos. The women's outfits were reminiscent of Europe in days gone by. The men wore dinner jackets and smoked.

There was no news from Poland which was in ruins. There were no gaps in the Iron Curtain.

Do not ask me how, because no-one ever told me. There was no time. Suddenly, the information came that someone, I do not know who, had seen a face in distant Krakow. It appeared to be the fake Major, who had been blown up by the canons of a panzer so many years earlier.

No-one takes any notice of small boys on these occasions. I was oblivious. I was oblivious as people murmured around me. Maybe I was oblivious because I was more interested in my next game of button football. I was oblivious until I realised my parents were packing their bags and leaving.

The Super Constellations of those bygone days flew out of Congonhas. I remember my father wearing a hat. I have no recollection of my mother. The family were out in force, watching from the picket-fenced garden where those who stayed behind could see those who were departing, provided they could stand the unbearable noise of the four propellers that gradually deafened the onlookers. The wind they caused was like a cyclone.

From here on I was absent. I was told some of the story; some of it I made up and part of it is the undeniable truth about new begin-

nings. I imagine the Krakow airport was little more than a shabby hangar. I know my father cried because he always did.

I know too that my mother had no idea what the father she had lost in her childhood would look like. The plane flew in from Germany or Switzerland and the airport was busy. There were no connecting bridges. They went down the stairs onto the tarmac and could see a crowd of indistinct faces in the distance, at the windows of the terminal. My mother wondered whether it would have been a good idea for her long-lost father to hold up a sign with the name of his long-lost daughter. I wonder if it is even possible to wonder in such a situation. I wonder what it was really like?

Long separations are explosively dramatic. When they culminate in a reunion, they are the infallible formula for raising the ratings of television programmes. They are used endlessly by fiction writers and rarely fail to touch readers. I suppose they are like palpable miracles. Reunions are like an incurable disease that is reverted or sight regained – the story ends, with an epilogue, bibliography and no more pages to read. And, inexplicably it begins again.

People react uncontrollably to episodes of this nature. They lack the capacity to understand because it is beyond cognitive boundaries. They cannot control their tears, sometimes they kneel, sometimes they seek refuge in scepticism.

However, the emotions of the protagonists of these poems are indecipherable.

What was going through the head of that girl who had died a thousand times and was now walking across the cemented ground of a strange airport?

What pleas rang in the ears of the old childless lawyer, his eyes fixed on the group walking towards him, still a formless body of people, but about to bring forth his daughter from another lifetime?

They found each other instantly, without a shadow of doubt or a second of hesitation. It was as though, startled, she had blinked and the horse was there once again, saddled and at the door.

They hugged each other, kissed and spoke sobbed whispers as they walked out of the building. It seemed as though they had suddenly been overwhelmed by a life or death urgency. My father held back, understanding the infinite urgency with which they had been struck.

I was told that the old fake Major almost ran out into the street with his daughter on his arm, pushing past people and knocking over suitcases on the way.

Booms, shouts, orders. Perhaps he was rescuing the little girl he left in Warsaw. Or maybe he was chasing the 30 years he had lost.

The cases were carefully placed in the boot of a small, clapped out East German car, a Trabant, and they set off at an imprudent speed.

I do not know what they talked about on the journey. There is always so much to tell a daughter who has been away for a week, but there is nothing to say to someone we have not seen for more than a quarter of a century. They probably made small talk and struggled with the language. My father said they looked at each other a lot, so much so that the journey was punctuated with braking and jolts.

My mother did not remember Krakow. Many years later she did not remember, except for fleeting scenes from her interrupted childhood.

When I was there reporting, I visited the city with extra attention and told her that I saw an overwhelmingly beautiful city that I had never known about. I found the house where she was born and other family references.

During my trip to Krakow there was one particular establishment that I asked about, in the remote hope that it had survived all the political and economic changes that had taken place since the reunion, four decades earlier. I did not even know its name. I was sure that if it still existed it would be in Rynek Glowny, the grandiose central square of the city, one of the largest in the European continent.

And that it would be a traditional restaurant where Polish people went at sunset to listen to music, dance and have dinner.

I found a place that fitted this description, still thriving, despite its age. Café Hawelka. I sat at a small side table, asked for a coffee and watched a live showing of the most touching scene I have never seen.

With the urgency that erupted in the airport and the same imprudence as the driving, they entered the café. There were three of them, but it seemed as though there were just two because at that moment my father was just an extra. She looked surprised. The journey had been long and that was not her reunited father's home. They sat down, ordered and a small orchestra started playing a waltz.

Dressed in his best suit, the Krakow lawyer and former fake Major stood up and with a gesture and tears in his eyes – I could not see very well from my table at a distance of forty years – he took his daughter in his arms and led her to the dance floor and the music.

The next day, after sleeping in the bedroom of my grandfather's new house (he would not have it any other way and had prepared everything to make his only daughter feel at home), my mother woke up with a start. Leaning on the end of the bed, where she and my father were resting after their long journey, stood a man whose heart had softened and who could hardly believe the twist his life had taken.

Later that same day, Teodor (now Tadeusz) took the couple who had travelled from afar to look around the city, see the sights and to go back to places Krisia did not remember. The rediscovery had worked out, in both real and emotional terms. The grandfather I never met (he died two months before my planned trip to Poland in the winter of 1972) was a citizen of some standing in the city from what I heard. He had come close to being the mayor of the city. I have no idea how this would have been possible at that time.

He was the lawyer of the Krakow Metropolitan Curia and was in regular contact with the archbishop of the city, Karol Wojtila, who was promoted years later to the papacy, under the name John Paul II. It is said that they were friends and confidantes.

One evening, the grandfather I only saw in photographs decided to honour the visitors by opening a rare liqueur from the Vatican cellar that he had been given by a cardinal friend. My father who was never a good drinker but was always good at displaying his emotions picked up his glass and when he heard the cue of the typical Polish toast *Na zdrovie!* emptied his glass in one gulp.

It went down in family folklore that, although intimacy between father and son-in-law was still in its early days, the Polish lawyer made the following comment and burst out laughing: "There is a saying in Poland that goes like this: You should give a wristwatch to a labourer, not a fine drink." My mother, infected by her father's humour, translated the sentence that had, of course, been uttered in the Slavic language. Sven, who was a natural joker, took it well and repeated the story whenever he got the chance until his death on All Souls' Day in 2000. He was 68 years old, and the likely cause of his death was septicaemia (general infection) due to the daily use of plastic probes to remove urine from his ineffective bladder.

19

A GAP IN THE STORY

There is no doubt that emotions are malleable. Those who provoke them, as I did in the previous chapter, may have the best intentions, but historical facts can still contradict them. While researching this story, I came across a piece of information that is potentially horrifying.

As I was going through a list of escapees on an internet site by the name of *alistadeschindler.com*, where I had found the hated Uncle Ferdynand and other people who left my mother and my grandmother behind in the camp at Plaszów, I came across a name that should not have been there. As clear as day. Name: Perlberger, Teodor, Jewish, Polish, born on 1897 and a "typist" according to the saviour's list.

My first impression was that it must be a coincidence – someone with the same name, although that was unlikely, someone who would have been about 46 or 47 years old when Oskar Schindler saved his Jews, eight years older than my grandmother Felicja who was left behind.

Perlberger roughly translates as "Mountain of Pearls". I later discovered that it is a common Jewish name in Poland (and in other Central European countries). On Schindler's official list was a Dora Perlberger, whose name appeared next to Teodor's. Maybe it was a sister of his I had never heard about, which also seems odd. His profession as it appeared on the list did not match Teodor's. Perhaps he was a lawyer, categorised as a typist to make it easier to include him in the profile of those who were to escape. Dora is down as a blacksmith. I have no doubt this is another trick to get past Goeth and his colleagues. But maybe the existence of a woman with the same surname increases the likelihood of it being a homonymy, as I suggested before.

What I do not understand – and never will – is that if the name on the list of those set free was indeed my maternal grandfather's, my mother would surely have harboured decades of hatred for him, rather than, as seen previously, for her Uncle Ferdynand. Could the lawyer turned major suddenly have returned to the story? If this proved to be the case, it would have numerous implications. Could it be that Teodor had abandoned his wife and his only daughter to the world of the condemned? Is it possible that he vanished with the rest of the family, leaving the most fragile people behind, his people?

I sorely regret not having the slightest idea what happened. I had never heard a single word about it, and there are no sources left for me to clear up the doubt. I try to place my bets on coincidence, that it was a different Teodor, just someone with the same name in the saddest of stories. It is plausible. I never heard my mother say anything about her father having abandoned her. I never saw an argument like the one between Krisia and her provisional mother in

Campos do Jordão, when she accused Uncle Ferdynand of being the worst enemy of the victims left behind in Plaszów.

I wonder whether Teodor was in another area of the camp and did not participate in the Lewcowicz's negotiations with Schindler and Goeth, so he was unaware of what was happening to my mother.

This would be a much more improbable escape valve given all the facts that led to the reunion described in the previous chapter.

Uncertainty, I assure you, can change everything, even the affection that I believed I had for the Pope's lawyer who received my parents so warmly. If he really was a treacherous pustule who escaped in the hands of Schindler, I hope the liqueur from the Vatican cellar caused him horrendous haemorrhaging.

But this was not the message that my mother, delighted to see him again, passed on to us.

Even the distance between his disappearance and reappearance are difficult to fit into this inconvenient "truth"; actually, most of this account is. Why would he dance with a daughter he had left in a concentration camp at the mercy of her own perverse fate? Why would he have stood at the foot of her bed, enchanted, while she slept?

In the version I knew before I went rummaging in that wretched site, the major/lawyer fled the Germans, was taken prisoner by Soviet troops (who had a peace pact with the Nazis at that time) and ended up in the maximum-security prison he had been in charge of before the war. As such, Teodor was familiar with intricacies of its layout, and he managed to escape via a wing that the invaders were unaware of. And that was it.

That was all I was told. He reappeared in the story almost 30 years later to play a fundamental role in the cinematographic reunion recounted above.

The fact that his name is on Schindler's list changes everything. Or nothing, if there is some mistake that is alluding me.

One way or another, I feel as though a spirit from the past has smudged the emotions I have described and the lines I have written.

Doubt can be more pernicious than facts. To hide it from those who are accompanying this account could be of great significance. Or not. I leave you at liberty to draw your own conclusions.

20

THE GRANDCHILDREN OF THE HOLOCAUST

The winding paths of Krisia and Andor's story – both of whom survived Auschwitz – lead us to the unlikely marriage of Léa Stern and this author, both the expected offspring of an unexpected story, who met quite by chance. Despite being my parents' son, I have never been interested in the details of my religion. I never studied at Jewish schools, I do not speak Hebrew, except for a few words I have picked up, and until I got married, I had had only two experiences as a member of this people. I had studied the very tedious text that I had to read at my Bar Mitzvah, the parashah, in which I remember some mention of a zinc roof.

My teacher was called Birnbaum; he was a man with a vast belly and kind eyes who lived with his wife over a bakery. To be honest, I have more affectionate memories of the aroma of the bread that was being made on the ground floor than of the gift of learning. I ate the bread. I have to confess that this consisted of my learning words by heart, which I repeated in a strained voice until the day of the ceremony. That day I did indeed receive many presents and a party at my paternal grandparents' house.

My mother, as I have recounted, was the most Jewish member of the family and was the only one who would have insisted I follow the faith that had tortured her. I do not, however, remember Krisia feeling particularly emotional on the occasion.

She did not cry (I have already said that she never did), and I do not remember her making a speech at my Jewish coming of age either publicly or in private. I really think it was of little importance to her.

It was only much later that I was rather disappointed to realise that my existence in the people of Abraham, a miracle of survival and continuity on my mother's part, was far less remarkable than history demanded.

Sven, my father, a living poem, did cry for me, for my mother and for the entire thousand-year history of the people to which he belonged. People are like that – some express themselves more overtly, some less.

There was a second attempt to turn me into a Jew worthy of his ancestry. When I was 14 years old, I was sent to Israel. The trip included my first visit to Europe and three months of hard work harvesting oranges, pulling up potatoes and painting a fence around a large corral. My other daily obligations included a long stretch as the community dishwasher and another job, which I had to do at night to avoid getting pecked when I transferred hundreds (I think maybe thousands) of hens from their former perch to a newly built coop. It was solitary painful job because the hens, which were unhappy about moving house, fought back whenever possible. They came in batches of four, and I would hold them by their feet. The strongest ones would manage to lift themselves up and peck my hand. In defence, I jerked them back down without letting go of their legs. More than once this manoeuvre led to a bird breaking a leg, and then it was put to one side and served for lunch or dinner later on.

Officially this type of trip was a great choice of holiday because young travellers were able to see a bit of the world at a low cost, part of the expenses of the trip being paid for in work. In practice though it was a brazen Zionist call for young generations from diverse countries to settle the country, which was 21 years old at the time and was participating in one war after another.

I could not say how many of the 70 people in my group ended up abandoning Brazil to start a new life in the "promised land" as it is known. But I have never forgotten the unfamiliar sight of young Brazilians getting off the plane and kissing the dirty ground of the airport, as Pope John Paul II would always do in years to come.

Zionism is a movement that was born at the end of the 19th century and was created by the Hungarian, Theodor Herzl. The stated objective of the movement was to create a Jewish state in Palestine and in time settle a large number of Jewish people, if possible all Jewish people, in the region.

Until today, there are those who view Zionism as a spurious racist movement, which led this specific region of the Middle East into the state of war in which it has found itself since its existence was approved in a United Nations (UN) resolution in November 1947 in a session that was, by the way, chaired by the Brazilian Oswaldo Aranha. Eighteen of the 33 countries voted in favour of the birth of a Jewish state. A few months later, the British, who ruled the region, withdrew, and the Jewish people took control of the territory in 1948.

The creation of the State of Israel happened as a way of mitigating the guilt that the world felt after the extermination of six million people during the Holocaust. But the history goes back much further and derives from the fact that the Jewish people in the Diaspora who started to be expelled from their territories in the 6th century BCE (the date of the first of many diasporas throughout history) never had an easy life in the places to which they immigrated. It is known that persecution has been a constant in the story of the Hebrew people, many of whom started to settle in ancient Palestine at the end of the 1800s, in the wake of Zionist ideals.

At any rate, I felt no attraction to Israel. I really missed my parents though. It was on this trip that my mother and I exchanged the famous 73 letters I mentioned earlier. I could not wait to get back home to the field where we played with the Polish football (what a ball that was!) that my newfound grandfather had given me, back to my friends and of course back to Brazil, where Pelé, the star player on the team that I was – and still am – passionate about, was performing magic on the pitch.

My return from Israel marked the end of my Zionist experience, and the only links I maintained with Judaism were the few occasions I went to the synagogue, once or twice a year, always to honour the survival of my mother and my grandparents who settled here.

My future wife was even further from the origins of her father (her mother was a rarely practicing Catholic, from Iguape, on the south coast of São Paulo). Léa had met some Jewish people while she was studying at the Instituto Mackenzie (a Protestant school), had a name that meant "star" in German and had worked for a brief period at a large jeweller's, which, through pure coincidence, had the same name as hers, the now internationally famous H. Stern. There she would show trays of rings, earrings and bracelets to moneyed clients.

Despite her name, Léa was not Jewish, because in the Jewish tradition, the faith of the children is decided by maternal lineage. Léa was brought up in a family with no declared Jewish family members, as I said. They celebrated Christmas and Easter, which her mother loved, and she was baptised, although she does not remember where.

When we were dating, these matters were of no consequence, even to Krisia, who, being a survivor, could have become invested in preserving the Jewish ties of her family.

The first person to notice the seriousness of our relationship was my grandmother Rosel, the nurse from Berlin, born in Kiel, on the edge of the North Sea and who before the war was almost entirely unaware of her Semitic progeny (in fact, Rosel who was blond with blue eyes could easily have passed as an Aryan woman). She sat Léa down for a private conversation in which she emphasised the fact that her grandson was the single male successor of the dynasty and would therefore not be marrying a gentile – she did not use the pejorative expression *goi*, that is how most Israelis refer to those of other faiths. Rosel had a Germanic rigour in her delivery, and Léa did not put up any resistance to the idea of converting to fulfil the wishes of her future husband's family. She was not bothered one way or the other, nor was I.

Jewish people do not proselytise; they do try to attract or indoctrinate people who do not belong to their ancestral line – and this may be the best quality of the religion. Léa and I were ordered by the rabbi to do a course on the commandments according to the Torah, the history of the Jews and their rituals. I have to admit that she was a much more dedicated student than her future husband – and until today, she knows more on the subject than I do.

At the end of the course, we participated in two rituals. The first of these was dinner at the home of Rabbi Henry Sobel (and his wife, Amanda), from the Israelita Paulista Congregation, at which Léa had to respond to three questions posed by the rabbi and had to state three times that she wanted to become Jewish. As the rabbi and I knew each other through work (In our respective roles of rabbi and journalist, we had been together at many occasions, including the Ecumenical mass of Vladimir Herzog at the Sé Cathedral, also on trips and in interviews), there was no formality. Léa became Jewish even before her father had time to stop crying about the event. She was also submerged in a bathtub (*mikvah*) in the basement of the synagogue to complete her religious transformation. At least my grandmother was happy, my father too and, of course, Andor Stern, who was astonished at the unexpected return to his Jewish roots.

I have no memory of Krisia, the main character in this story, showing any sign of emotion. As she did throughout her life – former and latter – she simply accepted what was happening with a remoteness that is typical of those who have suffered from forced "proximity".

And so it was that on 11 April 1978, the day after her bridegroom had experienced (always at work) the emotion of being arrested in the morning and caught in crossfire in the evening, the marriage was consummated.

I will omit the somewhat disastrous details of the celebration at the request of the bride, but the fact is that on that night, two grandchildren of the Holocaust – Krisia and Andor being the children – created a new cell in the family.

21

HONEYMOON WITH A NAZI

On 14 May 1984, Walter Rauff was declared officially dead in Santiago de Chile. There is a black-and-white video on YouTube showing silent scenes of his funeral, with a surprising number of Nazi soldiers (or officers) paying their last respects, young people with their arms raised offering him a solemn heil Hitler, and every now and then, a swastika comes into view.

Of the numerous war criminals who took refuge in South America, Rauff definitely chose the most remote spot. His hideout from 1958 to 1979 was Chile's southernmost city, windy Punta Arenas on the Straits of Magellan, which had its glory days when it was the obligatory stopover port for vessels going from the Atlantic to the Pacific (and vice versa).

The city ran into problems in 1914 with the inauguration of the Panama Canal, which created an indispensable shortcut, reducing maritime routes by tens of thousands of kilometres depending on the origin and destination of each trip.

In the early years of his life (as far as is known), Walter Hermann Julius Rauff worked for the German navy. This is hard to verify given the old adage that a leopard does not change its spots.

His hideaway at the end of the Earth was not a bolthole chosen on the basis of fear. It seems that the controversial organisation that went down in history with the name Odessa (*Organisation der ehemaligen SS-Angehörigen,* which means "Organisation of Former SS Members") had something to do with it. Although many scholars insist that Odessa never existed, there are numerous witnesses who say this organisation helped and supported former members of the SS, particularly in South America.

Its purpose was to hide, protect and disguise fugitives, almost all of whom were guilty.

Its participation in Rauff's destination is merely speculation and derives from the fact that he settled in such a remote place. However, he occupied a position of leadership in a company called Pesquera Magallanes, which caught, processed and canned the large, highly prized crabs of the region, known as *centollas.* Moreover, Walter Rauff had been a prominent Nazi figure, having worked closely with Reinhard Heydrich, a main architect of the Final Solution – an additional reason he would have earned the protection of the Odessa if it did actually exist.

Rauff's story is one of the many that have already ended, usually silencing secrets that will never be revealed. This is how History, with a capital H, works. Facts that cease, explanations not given, tormentors and victims who, at the end of the day, disappear from sight. There are people who try to retell it, but every account is a flawed version in one way or another. The points of view of the conqueror and the conquered oppose each other. A well-known quotation of Paul Valéry says:

"War is a massacre of people who don't know each other, for the profit of people who know each other but don't massacre each other." Obviously, he is referring to politicians and governors in the second part of the sentence and to soldiers and innocent people in the first. We can only speak of "profit" if we are going to learn lessons from war and not repeat it. So many wars in the history of humanity have occurred that it is impossible to count them. We have profited from none of them, and no matter what anyone says, conflicts continue to happen, their causes repeat themselves and there is no sign this situation will ever change.

Walter Rauff only appears here because he played a role in the story of Krisia, Andor and their successors – along with many others mentioned in previous chapters.

On our turbulent honeymoon in Chile, we encountered Augusto Pinochet's curfew and hostile street patrols. We spent some daunting days in Santiago and others filled with great beauty in Puerto Varas and Perto Montt in the midst of Swiss landscapes, volcanoes, lakes and mountains. Of course, the curfew was imposed in these places, too, but now looked like a comical backdrop to a musical. Then there was our bold adventure to the extreme south, almost 1,400 kilometres of sheer thrill for the young newlyweds. (Perhaps being newlyweds was the reason for our courage.)

Nobody went on holiday to this part of the world in 1978. We did, and it was just to be adventurous. We had seen photos somewhere of a stunning place that hardly anyone had heard of – Torres del Paine. It had been designated a nature reserve the same year we married, but at that time had no infrastructure. We had only a vague idea of how to get there, but we risked everything, and it worked out. In winds that threatened to turn over the hired Opala whenever we stopped – because of a flock of sheep, thousands of them weathering the gusts of southerly winds – we came across the strange peaks in the middle of the Patagonian plains. That must be the most tremendous view anyone could ever see in a lifetime.

The irresponsible, daring young bridegroom had read somewhere that Walter Rauff lived on the banks of the Strait of Magellan. Uncertain whether it would be possible to actually find him and undaunted by the consequences, he took his young 19-year-old wife on the adventure I describe here:

Why would a couple of honeymooners risk such a dangerous adventure? Looking back to 1978, I can find no response to this that is unrelated to innocence and irresponsibility. Our destination was Torres del Paine, in the far south of Chile. It was not well known at that time.

On 18 April 1978, exactly one week after our wedding, my wife, Léa, and I were freezing in Punta Arenas. It was cold and very windy in Chile's southernmost city, on the banks of the Strait of Magellan. My wife was not yet nineteen years old, neither was she afraid. It never crossed our minds that our marriage may be condemned to be one of the briefest of all times. Fear does not stick to people who are in love and idealistic, and they are always prepared to take challenges to the next level.

It was a simple idea – before heading for Torres del Paine, I would photograph and interview Walter Hermann Julius Rauff, a high-ranking war criminal. The famous Nazi hunter Simon Wiesenthal had announced months earlier that Rauff lived in that place at the end of the Earth. Curiously, no-one had got to him yet. And it would be stupid for a young husband to attempt this dubious precedent.

Dubious and unlikely. Rauff would probably not be in his Gestapo uniform, in the Plaza Muñoz Gamero, the most important square in the city. He probably went by the name of Pablo or Jaime to blend in with the local people. And he would probably be very wary of his own safety.

This is what would be expected of a man who carried the burden of over one hundred thousand deaths of civilians during the Nazi regime and who had been Heydrich's right-hand man. Nowadays, Heydrich is considered to be the cruellest of all the Nazi murderers. Rauff was responsible for speeding up the mass extermination process. It was taking too long in the eyes of the Nazi commanders. Being the diligent engineer that he was, he invented a lorry with the exhaust pipes turned inwards, also known as mobile gas chambers. With horrific finesse, these formidable machines were capable of executing a hundred people every ten minutes. It was a brainwave. If carbon monoxide was capable of killing absent-minded people who closed their garage doors and left the car engine running, obviously by creating a bend in the exhaust pipe and pointing it into a closed van, the effect would be even more potent.

For some instinctive reason (probably for lack of any other option), however, I took the most elementary precaution possible. I opened the telephone book of that windy city and looked up the letter R. There it was – not just Rauff, but H.J.W. Rauff.

This was when the opening line came to me for the report that I wrote in the same year for the now-extinct magazine, Status:

"To say that Hermann Julius Wagner Rauff's sleep is disturbed by ghosts is a stretch of the imagination."

A man who did not even go to the trouble of changing his name, despite being mentioned on lists of important Nazi criminals, must be confident about his impunity.

I immediately picked up the phone and asked for Don Walter. No, he wasn't there, but he would be back soon. "Could you tell me where I have called?" I ventured. The employee did not miss a beat. "A crab factory", she explained. It was the Industria Pesquera Magallanes, who provided tinned crab to Camelio. It was actually a fishing company, that specialised in catching the king crabs typical of the region. In fact, it was the biggest in that part of the world, with 13 large boats and the infrastructure to clean the crustaceans and put them in tins for exportation.

So, without any effort at all, I had the Nazi in the palm of my hand and I had my young wife at my side. An idealistic, reckless impetuosity was driving me towards the first report of worldwide interest of my career, supported unconditionally by the only person who should have been on the honeymoon with me.

Many Nazis, of all different ranks, sought refuge in South America after the war ended. Some even say that Hitler himself died in Villa la Angostura, in Argentina. Adolf Eichmann was caught in Buenos Aires by Israeli government agents; Klaus Barbie, the butcher of Lyon, was found in Bolivia; Joseph Mengele, the doctor who carried out horrendous genetic experiments in Auschwitz, drowned in Bertioga on the coast of São Paulo state. Presumably the list of Nazis that were never captured on the continent is even longer.

Dozens of fugitives were captured throughout the last century. Others lived in peace as though it were all water under the bridge.

Rauff was one of them, at least until 1978. I turned up without prior warning, notebook in one hand and an old Canon FTB in the other. The factory was on the Strait, six kilometres from the centre of Punta Arenas. There was a house at the front of the plot, with two angry dogs in it, baring their teeth. I thought it would be difficult to get in, but it was not. In the region of Patagonia, any real fear ended after the Panama Canal was created. All the ships that previously had to stop over at the port disappeared, leaving only solitude and decay.

This was all rather convenient for the génocidaire – welcome even. Rauff had become familiar with the city in 1925 (when it was prosperous), while on a Navy mission for his country. He thought it would be a good idea to return.

My wife waited for me in the almost brand new Brazilian Opala, parked outside the company, run by Rauff. As always, she was positive and expressed no concern at all, apart from hoping I would be able to do some good reporting. I met several smartly uniformed employees as I walked towards the main building. In response to my trivial questions about Don Walter, I heard only compliments. A good man and an excellent boss. Since he was widowed he had lived on site at the fishing company. Nothing was said about his past.

Actually, hardly any of those Chileans of humble origins had even heard of the world war, let alone the meaning of the word Holocaust.

Rauff hid away in Syria immediately after the war. He was a consultant to President Hosni Zaim and a spy acting against Zionist interests in the region. At the end of the fighting in Europe, he was the head of the Nazi military in the north of Italy with a record of massacres that is still untold today.

Everything I heard, however, over the high-pitched whistling of the Magellan winds, described a pleasant, kind gentleman. I decided to go in (how did I muster the courage?) and try to have the conversation I was hoping for. There was a reception desk at the top of a flight of stairs. I could see a bevelled glass fishbowl-style office, within which there was a shadow. It was definitely Rauff.

The man who spoke to me, by the name of Fernando, was the first person to show any hostility. He was probably uneasy about the camera hanging round my neck. I gave my name and requested an interview with the boss. Fernando's refusal was categorical.

"Don Walter never gives interviews!" My fear of being shot or something of the sort instantly fell away. I insisted. Fernando went into the glass room, came out and passed on the order. He asked me to leave.

But it's too late. I thought. I already have his address. I'll publish it. This could be an opportunity for him to give us his version.

Nothing. I sat on a chair in front of the desk in the hope of photographing the Nazi criminal should he leave his refuge, which he did in fact, about 40 minutes later. But the good assassin rushed past me with his hands over his face and went into the toilet before I could register anything.

I remembered my poor wife in the car being shaken about by the Patagonian wind and realised there was nothing more for me to do in that place. I had never been so close to an unadmonished génocidaire. Subsequently, in Brazil, I interviewed people from the Jewish community who belonged to the group called 'those who never forget'. Everyone knew who he was. One of them, who was of Italian origin, told me that in addition to inventing the deadly lorries, Rauff was also a cruel commander of the secret police in Milan and later, he was jointly responsible for the deaths of 2,300 Jewish Tunisians in a forced labour camp he was in charge of. In conversations and reading about him, I realised the risk I had run by taking him off guard. Information from the German intelligence itself showed that, behind the good-natured old man he seemed to be, Rauff was considered to have a short fuse, a bad character and was a contumacious drunk.

Maybe catching centollas *had pacified his character. Or maybe I had been lucky, which seems more likely to me.*

In the following year, I like to think that the report I published in 1978 was behind it, the Mossad agent, Yossi Chinitz reported an attempt to capture the creator of the death vans in the very place I had spent my honeymoon.

The release produced by the Israeli secret service at the time was written in advance and was leaked to the press.

"Today, in Chile, we have executed one of the biggest Nazi war criminals. In the Gestapo, he was responsible for designing the mobile gas chambers used to exterminate one hundred thousand Jewish people."

The plan failed because Rauff had already left the city, apparently under the protection of General Augusto Pinochet's own political police. Sources say that Rauff and his son, Walter Jr, worked for the Chilean dictator's political police, the DINA after he ended his career in fishing. In the following years, all attempts to extradite him were scuppered by Pinochet.

Rauff died on 14 May 1984, from a myocardial heart attack caused by the advance of lung cancer, aged 77. It cannot be said whether, at any time in his life, he felt afraid or remorseful. Certainly, he would not have been bothered about the foolish honeymoon couple who had surprised him six years earlier. Anyone who wishes to see the nefarious dazzle of his funeral – including Nazi salutes by friends, followers and young Nazis, can access the link https://www.youtube.com/watch?v= ngp6NQtVUtw. Part of which, by the way, was recently removed.

Léa and I celebrated our 44-year wedding anniversary in 2018. The trip to those distant Torres, at a time when they were protected merely by decree, without any of the entrances, fences

and guards it has nowadays, was unforgettable. Never again did
we chase after any kind of criminal. We understand these days
that honeymoons are meant to be for just two people.

My brief sighting of Rauff is not the only direct contact I
have had with war criminals in my adult life. In the same
year, the Brazilian police found Gustav Wagner, known as
the "Beast of Sobibor" who had also fled post-war Germany
to live in Brazil. He was more cautious than Rauff and
adopted the pseudonym of Günther Mendel and lived in
São Paulo. He had been a sergeant and second-in-command
at the Sobibor concentration camp. Jews, Soviet prisoners of
war and possible Romani were sent to Sobibor where they
were suffocated in gas chambers supplied by the exhaust
pipes of diesel engines – an evolution of Rauff's invention.
Around 260,000 people were killed using this weapon.

I met Wagner at a turbulent meeting that took place at
DOPS – the dreaded Department of Political and Social
Order of the Brazilian dictatorship. He was an exceptionally
large man and said hardly anything to the journalists. When
he did, it was with a pleasant smile, inviting empathy.

As there had been for Rauff, there was a request for his
extradition. Three countries wanted to put him to trial:
Austria, Germany and Israel. The Brazilian dictatorship,
which was aligned with the Chilean one, refused, alleging
that his crimes had already lapsed. Terrified by the possibility that the Brazilian government may change its mind
under international pressure, Wagner committed suicide in
the town of Atibaia in 1980.

Even today I am surprised by my detached emotional reaction in the presence of mass murderers, particularly in the
case of Rauff, as I was alone when I came so close to him. I
did not feel the urge to go for him or hit him, nor was I over-

come with hatred in the way some people must feel when they come face-to-face with cruel génocidaires. I did not feel sad or downcast, which would also have been quite under-standable.

I left the fishing complex, the dogs barking behind me, and saw my wife through the car window. She was smiling (because I had survived or because we were newlyweds?)

I once heard a psychiatrist say that people are either born to kill or not. Those who kill are usually psychopaths who start by taking one life and never stop. I am not one of these people. Rauff was.

22

THE LAST DEATH

There is no longer even the time to which she clung. The back room at the end of the corridor now observes the silence that Krisia practiced almost all her life. These days the silence is eerie. The moment that will never be forgotten is the last time my mother was in the room we had improvised for her to feel at peace, without the fear of the changes that had hounded her throughout her life.

It was quick, very quick and terrifying. Those who were there – my sister, my wife, a carer who used to spend the weekends with her and me – will never forget.

Krisia was on the floor, it was impossible to lift her up. Her hands trembled; her eyes moved in a strange way. The ambulance woman, paramedic or nurse, I do not know, said that her pulse was slow, and her other vital signs were deteriorating fast. She called to the driver for help.

The television was not on and her wristwatch, a Champion with a large face, was on the table. She was not worried about the time now, and she did not ask for it to be placed on her thin wrist. Her eyes moved back and forth, although they were not looking for anyone or anything. Her body was limp, which meant her weight had spread.

With the dexterity of people who are accustomed to handling this kind of situation, the ambulance driver and the woman rolled Krisia up in a bedspread and took her, like a corpse, out through the garden into the bright light that she had always avoided.

I accompanied the movement of the bulging bedspread out to the car that was emblazoned with the red cross that has appeared so many times throughout this story. Evidence that the end was near seemed unequivocal, but I held onto the certainty that Krisia would recover. It is the nature of survivors to survive, and she would do so once again. At least that was what I wanted, and I wanted it very much, in spite of everything. Even if she would no longer be able to read a single word of the books she used to devour when she could see and reason. Even if I had seen her beg for it all to be over because she was not able to keep herself company anymore.

I confess I have always been selfish in this sense, and I tried to see hope in the sparks of awareness, some of which were even good-humoured. I would glare at the well-intentioned people who said, so many times, that it was good that Krisia could finally rest.

Good? For whom? As far as I knew, only her worst executioners had deemed it good that she should cease to live.

The fact is though that the few emotions she felt had started to disappear, and I do not know – because she was unable to say – whether, worse than anything, the time had come that she had forgotten everything, maybe even the memory of captivity, pain, yelling and threats.

I think it was Andor who once referred to the guilt of having survived. It is as though you see the world falling apart around you, the universe shrouded in smoke and fog, the final cries ceasing, as are the gunshots and the moans. And then, sooner or later, the wind carries it all away. Then there is nothing and nobody. Those you cared for and those you hated have all disappeared, all at once.

Suddenly, it is just you. Somehow you have to lift yourself up, if you can. And then you have to walk, even though you have no idea where to. You are thirsty, and there is water somewhere. Now you can drink as much as you want, until your thirst is quenched, in a way you cannot remember happening in many years.

The water sweeps away the delirium and brings back some reasoning. It is time to realise you exist. You have been left behind. You are saved.

Finally, the worst – it is time to wonder why. Why only you? Who decided that it was fair that you should carry on? How many people died (or was it you who killed them?) so your life, only yours, could carry on?

And a conclusion is reached that is more painful that any of the whippings you endured, the stones you had to carry, the bodies you saw piled up and all the loved ones who you saw disappear.

What did I do wrong?

Guilt, guilt is sticky. It does not come out in the wash.

They say that guilt is impregnated in the souls of the perse-cuted. People who are Jewish, in faith, ethnicity or heritage, usually carry it. If this deduction is correct and survival does lead to this feeling, the peoples who have produced survivors throughout the ages will also be the ones who bequeath humanity to those who carry a strong sense of guilt.

Guilt.

Some reallocate it. They accuse their neighbours, the regime, the times, the others. Others carry the burden because they feel that they are eternally responsible for continuing a story that should have ended. I do not know how to evaluate which is more honest or elevated, whether it is to reallocate it or to carry it.

I know, however, that guilt itself is the result of such an intense emotional turmoil that it warrants no judgment.

Maybe Pavel, whom I spoke about in earlier pages, freed himself when he killed his tormentors. Are revenge and redemption compatible?

We are always pursuing both – either seeking revenge on those who throw stones or forgiving ourselves for not doing so.

The Way of Saint James (Camino de Santiago), for example (and the other ways that lead to the Compostela Cathedral), is always full of pilgrims in search of redemption. There are those who imagine that each step towards being forgiven is made with contrition. I have heard many accounts – including those made by journalists I have sent there to do reporting – that prove the opposite. The closer people come to forgiveness, the more they sin. As people draw closer to forgiveness, they feel free to sin and by sin I mean any behaviour that the person seeking redemption considers to be wrong, no matter what their belief system may be.

The Camino de Santiago has lust, betrayal, greed, rage and evil. It even has guilt – but it does not have fear because at the end of it, there will be unconditional forgiveness.

In Judaism, one day a year is dedicated to forgiveness. It is the most sacred day, the aforementioned Yom Kippur. It does not matter how big the mistake was that the believer committed, on that day, if the precepts are honoured – fasting, prayers and homage to those who have passed – God will forgive.

However, for those who carry the kind of guilt that only survivors nurture, even when they are blameless, there is no reprieve.

Today I wonder how much of this kind of harmful blameless guilt existed in Krisia's silence, in Pavel's gunshot and in Andor's loquaciousness.

And how much indulgence exists in the true guilt of the tormentors?

The last day of my mother's life was long.

For 14 hours she had to be in the hands of doctors, whom she had never liked. I remember that on the day Sven passed away, I arrived at the hospital and saw his wife insulting the doctor with a rare virulence. She knew him; she had played tennis with him. I believe that, as she did on many other occasions throughout her life, she projected onto that doctor her own inability to accept death, wretched death that would not leave her alone.

Although she always respected the men in white coats, in the depths of her soul, she hated their omnipotence, the absolute irrefutable power they always exuded.

My mother spent years of her life reading stories – novels and tales – about doctors, their errors, virtues and talents.

On that sunny Sunday (yes, it was Sunday, and it was hot, which she had always detested), Krisia was uselessly subjected to hospitals, ambulances, a variety of tests, kind people and quite unkind people. I saw her again in the early hours of Monday, pale under the green light of the Intensive Care Unit. Although she was weak, I thought her eyes met mine one last time. "Silly Mum," I whispered. "You always put up with everything. Keep going."

Someone, I did not see who, pulled the bed and took her to fit a catheter, paramount, according to the doctor, and who could argue with an omnipotent being?

I needed to tell every word I wrote in this book, for the first time, for a number of reasons. One of them, although tardy, was so those men dressed in pale green would know whom they were dealing with. She was not any old patient. She was Krisia, who had survived a thousand times, Krisia.

Half an hour later, maybe 40 minutes, my sister, my son, my nieces and nephews, and I were sitting in a room that was smarter than the occasion demanded. It was light and spacious with stone (maybe marble?) like that which lines the walls of hotels. We were like a flock of little open-mouthed birds in that big room.

Then two doors opened, and a committee made up of three men and a woman emerged. I did not think about it at the time, but now I know their names: Goeth, Schindler, Fredek and Margot.

Four of my mother's tormentors, ready to announce, "You know, yes, she was weak, we did all we could, she had a cardiac arrest, it's not good news."

The chorus of death.

The quartet did not know, but they had just executed a survivor, without malice, and maybe they had even acted with professional perseverance, but that was what had happened.

I had the reaction she would have had. I became angry; I was unpleasant to people who did not deserve it and went outside to walk a little in the humid night air. I could not help noticing that the heat was reminiscent of an open furnace.

⁂

A message from the Author

Before you go, I'd like to ask you for a little favour.

If you enjoyed this book, please don't forget to leave a review on Amazon! It only takes a minute. I highly appreciate your input.

Authors very much depend on reviews to attract new readers. I would greatly appreciate it if you'd share your experience of reading my book by leaving your review on Amazon. It doesn't have to be long. A sentence of two would do nicely.

PHOTOGRAPHS

*Felicja Perleberger, Krisia's mother, who died on the day
Bergen-Belsen was liberated*

Teodor Perlberger, Krisia's father

Krisia and her father, Teodor, in Krakow, before the war

Krisia (the smallest child) with part of the Lewcowicz family, before the war

Krisia with her dog in Krakow, one year before the outbreak of WW2

Bergen Belsen: liberation day, 1945. Survivors were put together in a hall. Krisia (encircled), in the middle of the picture

In Malmö, Krisia with someone of the sanatorium (1946)

*Left to right: Teodor Perlberger, Krisia and her husband
Sven in Krakow, circa 1965-1966*

Krisia with her son Ronny and her daughter Eliane, circa 1960

Krisia with her son Ronny and her daughter Eliane, circa 1960

Krisia

NOTES

11. The bright blue camp

1. In fact, this was true of photographic archives at the institution in its early days. Later, hundreds of other photographs started to emerge, through the direct collaboration of organisations and people, such as the British Army, the Red Cross and Zionist groups interested in taking survivors to Israel, in addition to photographs from other sources.

14. The Czech shot

1. https://pt.wikipedia.org/wiki/Document%C3%A1rio

ABOUT THE AUTHOR

Ronny Hein is a writer, journalist and publicist. He was born in Brazil in 1955, ten years after the end of the Second World War. He is the son and son-in-law of concentration camp survivors. The stories of both his mother and father-in-law, among others, are told in this eleventh book. Six of which have been published in Brazil.

As a journalist, he worked in television, radio and on newspapers and principally, magazines. He was a Director of the Brazilian edition of FORBES for four years, the Sunday magazine of the Jornal do Brasil and a number of others. His field of expertise, however, was in creating and directing travel magazines like Viagem e Turismo, Próxima Viagem, Caminhos da Terra, Top Destinos and Lonely Planet Brasil. In this role he had the opportunity to visit and write about 82 different countries.

As a publicist he was a copywriter at Delta Propaganda and a partner at Sven Hein & Associados Propaganda, both in São Paulo.

He has been awarded a number of prizes throughout his career, eight of which were from the European Tourism Commission. He also received a gold medal of merit from the French government for his contribution to publishing about tourism in France.

HOLOCAUST SURVIVOR MEMOIRS

The Series **Holocaust Survivor Memoirs World War II** , by Amsterdam Publishers, consists of the following autobiographies of survivors:

1. Outcry - Holocaust Memoirs, by Manny Steinberg

Amazon Link: getbook.at/Outcry

2. Hank Brodt Holocaust Memoirs. A Candle and a Promise, by Deborah Donnelly

Amazon Link: getbook.at/Brodt

3. The Dead Years. Holocaust Memoirs, by Joseph Schupack

Amazon Link: getbook.at/Schupack

4. Rescued from the Ashes. The Diary of Leokadia Schmidt, Survivor of the Warsaw Ghetto, by Leokadia Schmidt

Amazon Link: getbook.at/Leokadia

5. My Lvov. Holocaust Memoir of a twelve-year-old Girl, by Janina Hescheles

Amazon Link: getbook.at/Lvov

6. Remembering Ravensbrück. From Holocaust to Healing, by Natalie Hess

Amazon Link: getbook.at/Ravensbruck

7. Wolf. A Story of Hate, by Zeev Scheinwald with Ella Scheinwald

Amazon Link: getbook.at/wolf

8. Save my Children. An Astonishing Tale of Survival and its Unlikely Hero, by Leon Kleiner with Edwin Stepp

Amazon Link: getbook.at/LeonKleiner

9. Holocaust Memoirs of a Bergen-Belsen Survivor & Classmate of Anne Frank, by Nanette Blitz Konig

Amazon Link: getbook.at/BlitzKonig

10. Defiant German - Defiant Jew. A Holocaust Memoir from inside the Third Reich, by Walter Leopold with Les Leopold

Amazon Link: getbook.at/leopold

Forthcoming:

In a Land of Forest and Darkness. The Holocaust Story of two Jewish Partisans, by Sara Lustigman Omelinski

HOLOCAUST SURVIVOR TRUE STORIES

The Series **Holocaust Survivor True Stories WWII**, by Amsterdam Publishers, consists of the following biographies:

1. Among the Reeds. The true story of how a family survived the Holocaust, by Tammy Bottner

Amazon Link: getbook.at/ATRBottner

2. A Holocaust Memoir of Love & Resilience. Mama's Survival from Lithuania to America, by Ettie Zilber

Amazon Link: getbook.at/Zilber

3. Living among the Dead. My Grandmother's Holocaust Survival Story of Love and Strength, by Adena Bernstein Astrowsky

Amazon Link: mybook.to/ManiaL

4. Heart Songs - A Holocaust Memoir, by Barbara Gilford

Amazon Link: getbook.at/HeartSongs

5. Shoes of the Shoah. The Tomorrow of Yesterday, by Dorothy Pierce

Amazon Link: getbook.at/shoah

6. Hidden in Berlin. A Holocaust Memoir, by Evelyn Joseph Grossman

Amazon Link: getbook.at/HiddenBL

7. Separated Together. The Incredible True WWII Story of Soulmates Stranded an Ocean Apart, by Kenneth P. Price, Ph.D.

Amazon Link: getbook.at/SeparatedTG

8. The Man Across the River: The incredible story of one man's will to survive the Holocaust, by Zvi Wiesenfeld

Amazon Link: getbook.at/ZviWi

9. If Anyone Calls, Tell Them I Died, by Emanuel (Manu) Rosen

Amazon Link: getbook.at/EMrosen

10. The House on Thrömerstrasse. A Story of Rebirth and Renewal in the Wake of the Holocaust, by Ron Vincent

Amazon Link: getbook.at/RVincent

11. Dancing with my Father. His hidden past. Her quest for truth. How Nazi Vienna shaped a family's identity, by Jo Sorochinsky

Amazon Link: getbook.at/DancingJS

12. The Story Keeper. Weaving the Threads of Time and Memory, a Memoir, by Fred Feldman

Amazon Link: getbook.at/StoryKeeper

Printed in Poland
by Amazon Fulfillment
Poland Sp. z o.o., Wrocław

90060850R00110